MW00584243

SPIRALING LIFE FORCE PRESS

Experiencing God's Reflection

COPYRIGHT © 2012 BY LYN DILBECK

Experiencing God's Reflection;
The Role Qi Gong Plays in the Transformation of Consciousness

Cover Design: Peggy Sands, Indigo Disegno

Design, Photography, Illustration: Peggy Sands, Indigo Disegno

Back cover Photo: Pam Taylor

Typesetting: Ingrid Hardy

No part of this book
may be used, reproduced or transmitted
in any form by any means, electronic or mechanical, including pho-
tocopying and recording or by any information storage or retrieval
system, in any manner except in the case of brief quotations embodied
in critical articles and reviews. Request for such permission should be
submitted in writing to the author.
Spiraling Life Force • www.spiralinglifeforce.com

All rights reserved.
Printed in the United States of America.
First Edition December 21, 2012

ISBN: 978-0-9885414-1-2

Table of Contents

PART I

PART II

DEDICATION AND ACKNOWLEDGEMENT

This book is dedicated to God Our Mother; who is the Qi; who is the Divine Intelligence and Power of Creation; who is the Holy Spirit bringing to us, in each of our experiences, our reawakening.

<hr/>

I want to give thanks to all of my Sisters and Brothers who have helped make this book possible, starting with my parents, Barbara and Will Baty and Jerry and Patricia Dilbeck. Thank you Gwen for being an embodiment of the Mother for me, and I give thanks to Josephine Taylor and Doug for opening the door for me to metaphysics.

I thank my family of friends and students for supporting me through the years and my teachers who have challenged me to go within and shared with me their experiences along the inner path.

Special thanks to Peggy Sands for your artful eyes and generosity, and to Ingrid Hardy for your precision and steadfastness.

Thank you Master Li for showing me the heart of Qi Gong Practice.

AUTHORS NOTE

For most of my life, and I know that I am not alone in this, I've carried this feeling that we are bigger and life is deeper than what we are now experiencing. I have hungered to know who we really are as the family of humankind, and who I am as an individual person. This feeling and hunger are a living force within me that have always influenced how I choose to invest my life force and time. More and more I am allowing this force to guide the direction of my life.

I have trusted what I have experienced and what I have learned from the places, books, and people to which my questing has taken me. I have trusted the spiritual practices that have come to me: meditation, internal martial arts, and Qi Gong. I have trusted my desire to teach these arts. And now here I am, trusting this desire to write about all that has been shown to me on this journey.

When I embarked on this endeavor, I thought, because I had practiced and taught Qi Gong for nearly 30 years, I could easily write about how to do Qi Gong Practice and explain its many benefits. So I proceeded to create an outline that included these two statements: "In its essence, the practice of Qi Gong is spiritual", and "The Practice of Qi Gong is simply a conscious conversation between human beings and the intelligent power of all Creation, Qi."

As I began to focus on the writing, it just hit me that lying beneath these two sentences was a profound belief system, or a story. Frankly, at that point I was overwhelmed and confused for even though I wholeheartedly felt that these statements were my truth, coming from many years of meditation and Qi Gong Practice, I did not know if I really knew this story.

It was then clear to me that I could not continue to write about how to do Qi Gong without first rediscovering this story. The pages that follow are this story ~ a system of beliefs I needed to remember and share.

Lyn Dilbeck
December 12, 2012

remember Who We Are. This is the reason we walk the inner path, and it is the primary intention of Qi Gong Practice.

It is my prayer that through your experience of this story, you are inspired to find within your own story the deep sense of being the Oneness and Love of God that you and I have always been.

This story brings forth many philosophical concepts that form the basis of Qi Gong theory. In the practice of Qi Gong, understanding this theory is one of the ways our mind gives itself unto our oneness, and is as essential to the transformation of our consciousness as every other level of the practice. Our reasons for even engaging in Qi Gong Practice, especially as westerners, first come to us through our Mental Altar or Tan Tien. Understanding the theory of Qi Gong also plays a huge part in birthing the motivational power needed to actualize or bring into manifestation the spiritual intention of the practice.

One example of this is that in Qi Gong theory, we are not created as an internally divided being; we are the embodiment of oneness. We also are not, nor were we ever, separate from God, and we do not exist separate from Creation, all life forms, and one another ~ we exist in oneness.

It is through our mind, our Mental Tan Tien, that we

first "see" or have awareness of this oneness. For this is the highest function of our mind, to give us a clear, mental reflection, or thought experience, of our Spiritual Heart. This heart is where the Oneness and Love we share with God, Creation, and each other is forever present. It is in our conscious experience of this mental reflection that we come to know again that our enlightenment or awakening arises from and is the complete integration of all the levels and pieces of our being.

This understanding through our mind is then what motivates us to consciously reunite our mind, heart, body, consciousness, and Soul. Allowing this oneness to reform within us is our spiritual healing and the return of Christ to this earth.

WHO WE ARE

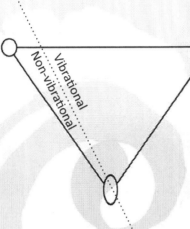

The One Source Creator of All (God)

- Oneness and Love
- Infinite potential (all possibilities)

Vibrational
Non-vibrational

Creation or Qi

- Forces of yin Qi and yang Qi
- Divine Intelligence of God within Creation
- Intelligence and medium that brings the infinite potential of God into vibrational existence
- Intelligence and medium of movement (power)
- Intelligence and medium that allows us as consciousness to experience what we choose to hold onto as our truth

Consciousness (Life)

- God's faculty of perception
- God's ability to consciously experience
- The conscious expression of love as both giving and receiving
- Choice

THE FIRST PART
of the
THREE PART STORY

Who I Am

WITHIN EACH OF US

THIS STORY MOVES IN THE MYSTICAL nothing-and-everything we call God or Spirit. This unknowable, undefinable nothing-and-everything is beyond all concepts or thinking, emotions and feeling, energy and matter, time and space. And yet, absolutely everything that exists, including us, is suppose to come forth from this One God.

So, in order to even tell this story, I had to find somewhere within this nothing-and-everything a place to begin. I therefore gave God a state of being called Oneness and a doing called Love. And so the story begins with the Oneness of God Loving.

God is Oneness. Love is the Oneness of God giving itself. The way Oneness loves is to give all of itself. So the One Spirit of God chose to love, to give all of itself. This action of love became the act of creating, and through this action, all Creation came into being.

Because God's Love is complete giving of oneself, Creation is the extension of God. Therefore, Creation, too, is the Oneness and love of God.

God is Oneness. Love is the Oneness of God giving itself. Because God's Love is complete giving of oneself, Creation, too, is the Oneness and Love of God.

But in order for Creation to come into being, the One Spirit of God chose to divide itself into a trinity of forces.

God Our Mother or Creation is this Trinity, the yin Qi, the yang Qi, and a third omniscient, omnipresent, and omnipotent intelligence. This intelligence is the extension of God's intelligence throughout Creation and is the intelligence holding the forces of yin and yang in their union of supreme balance. This union of balance is God's Oneness in vibrational form.

In the balance formed from and by the Trinity of God Our Mother, a perfect mirror forms that, upon receiving God, brings the reflection of all that is God into manifestation, into vibrational existence. This image of God is the entirety of Creation.

At this point, we come to a revealing passage in this story for God is Oneness, but the reflection in the mirror is infinite realities made of infinite manifesting possibilities. Therefore, within the Oneness of God there is infinite potential, infinite beliefs and stories. The entirety of

Creation, the actual existence of infinite realities and infinite possibilities, is the reflection of these infinite beliefs and stories of God.

Of course, this is a love story. The One Spirit of God, through love, creates God Our Mother. She is the entirety of Creation with her infinite body, power, and intelligence. To her, the One Spirit has given all of itself, Oneness and Love. Therefore, being Oneness and Love, God Our Mother also now seeks to give all of herself. It is in their union, the union created from the complete giving of themselves to one another, that a most holy child is conceived within her body. This child is Christ.

As if the story wasn't big enough at this point, with the creation of Christ the story explodes beyond infinity. And yet Christ brings this story to the very center of the human heart, for we are Christ. We, as Christ, are the Oneness and Love of both God and Creation. We are the infinite potentials, the infinite beliefs and stories of God, and we are the infinite realities of Creation, all in an individualized being. The birth of Christ actualizes, or makes real, the most beautiful potentials of God. These are the precious gifts Christ brings into Creation:

- The Gift of Conscious Experience
- The Transformation of Love
- The Gift of Life
- The Gift of Choice

Conscious Experience

Without Christ there is no experiencer, no "I Am" point of reference from which to perceive and interact with Creation from inside Creation. As an individualized being, Christ becomes this experiencer, this "I Am" presence. Christ becomes the very ability to have conscious experience.

Being Oneness and Love, God Our Mother also now seeks to give all of herself. It is in the union created from the complete giving of themselves to one another, that a most holy child is conceived.

Christ lives within Creation, consciously experiencing the reflections of God that form all realities. Christ's ability to consciously experience these reflections in the Qi of Creation (and in the Qi of his or her body) becomes God and Creation's ability to consciously experience one another. Christ's experiences are God and Creation's experiences for God and Creation are within Christ.

Christ is the holy vessel in which God, Creation, and the Consciousness of Christ are one. We, as Christ, are the ability to consciously experience this oneness, the oneness we share with God, Creation, all life forms, and each other.

Transformation of Love

Being the ability to consciously experience, Christ transforms love. Through love, God and Creation have given all of themselves to Christ. Christ is God (our soul) and Creation (our body) and, through the gift of conscious experience, Christ is God and Creation's ability to consciously experience one another. God, through Christ, consciously experiences its reflection in Creation. In this experience, God receives himself and receives Creation's love. Creation, too, through Christ, consciously experiences herself and experiences God as he is experiencing her. Through this experience, Creation receives herself and receives God's Love. In Christ, love is no longer just the giving of oneself, but is transformed into the giving and receiving of oneself. Christ completes the circle of love. Through Christ's experiences, the giving of oneself becomes the receiving of oneself ~ giving and receiving become one action.

Christ also transforms love through his or her everyday experiences of life. As an individual being, Christ experiences Creation from his or her unique perspective surrounded by all of the other life forms and things in Creation. But at the same time Christ is the living knowledge that there is but one Spirit and that everything that exists is unified through this Spirit. Being this knowledge, Christ shares him or her self with all of the life forms and things within Creation. In this sharing, Christ experiences Creation's love; Creation's giving of herself. All that Christ gives to Creation is returned to Christ in the form of Christ's conscious experience of her.

Christ Consciousness is the living experience of giving all of oneself and receiving all of oneself. In sharing ourselves with Creation and our brothers and sisters, we,

God, and Creation receive ourselves. This is the wisdom of Love.

Life

Christ is all life and the culmination of life. Christ is the infusion of unknowable God into Creation. This union of God within Creation creates and is life ~ the intelligent movement within Creation propelling her toward an awakened awareness of Oneness and Love.

Life is the One Spirit of God, and the Divine Intelligence and Power of God Our Mother bringing together the elements (the matter and energies) of Creation into the most sacred geometries. These geometries form the organic systems that support life. Under the guidance and timing of life, these systems evolve into the perfected, living temple, a body compatible with the Consciousness of Oneness and Love. This movement of life culminates in the consciousness and being of Christ and the perpetuation of Christ within Creation.

Choice

There are infinite beliefs and stories within the Oneness of God, and Creation is the infinite realities formed from the vibrational reflection (the manifestation) of these beliefs and stories. Christ is the ability to consciously experience any and all of these infinite beliefs and stories as the reflections forming Creation.

But Christ also is the power to choose which of these

infinite beliefs and stories will become his or her conscious experience. Christ is the gatekeeper of all beliefs and stories. What Christ chooses to believe in or chooses to hold onto as his or her truth becomes Christ's conscious experience of Creation, or Christ's reality.

Spirituality Is Our Oneness

God is Oneness, One Spirit. Love is the Oneness of God, sharing itself. It is through God's Love that the One Spirit of God is in all Creation and in us. When you are Oneness, it is Oneness that you share by way of Oneness. You share all of Who You Are so that all of Who You Are extends as Oneness. This is the way of God. This is the quality of Love. Through Love, Oneness begets Oneness.

Through Love, the One Spirit of God extends itself as Creation and also extends itself into each one of us as our Soul. The Oneness of God is the Oneness in all Creation; it is the Oneness in each human being, and it is the Oneness uniting God, Creation, humans, and all life forms.

Creation is the manifesting reflection of God. But for God to extend into vibrational form, the One Spirit of God divides itself into the forces of yin Qi and yang Qi. It is in the supreme balance that forms as these forces give and receive one another completely, that the image of God appears and the Oneness of God is shared. This supreme balance between the yin Qi and yang Qi is the Oneness and Love of God reflecting into Creation as the Love and Divine Intelligence of God Our Mother.

God Our Mother is the yin Qi, yang Qi and this omniscient, omnipresent, and omnipotent intelligence orchestrating the balance in these forces. This Sacred Trinity of Qi forms and sustains everything in Creation from atoms to galaxies and all expressions of life.

God Our Mother also is the energy, matter, and intelligence forming our human body. This is the holiness of our body ~ each one of us is a perfect microcosm of all Creation (the macrocosm). It is through this understanding that we find the inner path of our awakening or enlightenment.

Metaphysics teaches that the entirety of Creation exists in three levels: the Causal, Astral, and Etheric (the Etheric level consists of energy and matter). Our body is a holy temple to all of Creation, holding within it the altars of these realms. In Qi Gong Practice these are the Upper, Middle, and Lower Tan Tiens or "energy fields". These tan tiens or altars vibrate within us as our mental, emotional, and energy/physical bodies and also manifest within us as our brain, heart, and kidneys (also adrenals). Each altar is formed from the interplay of the yin and yang forces of Qi and each altar has its own vibrational spectrum, much like an octave in music. In the lower frequencies of their particular spectrum, the tan tiens form our organs, in their middle frequencies they form our bodies (mental, emotional & energetic/ physical), and in their higher frequencies they are the heavenly realms or planes of all Creation.

God Our Mother is Qi. And in the Practice of Qi Gong, it is with her that we are consciously conversing on every level of our being and every level of Creation. She is reminding us that Creation and we are the extensions of the One Spirit of God, and through love, the One Spirit, Creation and all life forms are one. This is Who We Are, this is our deepest core truth, and this is the meaning of spirituality.

What Is Qi?
What Is Gong?

God is Oneness and Love. Motivated by Love, God gives its Oneness and Love completely. This extension of God's Oneness and Love is the creation of Qi.

Qi comes forth from God as the feminine aspect of God:
- Qi is God become manifest
- Qi is God Our Mother in whom all the energy, matter, and intelligence of Creation exists
- Qi is Creation in all her form and function
- Qi forms our temple or being and our three, sacred altars of thought, feeling and emotion, energy and matter.

In the Christian trinity of God, Qi is the Holy Spirit.

As was shared in the creation story, for God to become Creation, the One Spirit divides itself into the most holy trinity of God Our Mother. She is the forces of yin Qi and yang Qi and the manifesting intelligence of Oneness and Love ~ the extension of God intelligence into Creation. Being this intelligence, God Our Mother coordinates the interaction between the yin Qi and yang Qi, overseeing their complete and balanced giving and receiving of one another. This balance is how the Oneness and Love of God extends itself to become Creation. It is within this balance that the image of God, and therefore the image of God's infinite potential, appears as infinite, manifesting realities.

Qi is the foundational trinity, setting the pattern for all Creation, each thing in Creation, and each life form:

- The whole of Creation is a trinity formed from the three vibrational planes or realms of Qi ~ the Causal, Astral, and Etheric.
- These three planes form the three bodies enveloping the individualized Soul of every human being, and also form the three tan tiens or altars within each of us.
- The design of Christ as the union of God, Creation, and Consciousness is a trinity.
- Each and every entity, organic and inorganic, comes into manifestation by way of the trinity pattern.
- The trinity of God Our Mother is the design and function of the multitude of systems that guide each thing, living and non-living, in its harmonious interaction with everything else.

One=Three/Three=One is the equation of God extension. It is also the equation of our return to God. This partnership of Oneness, formed through the balance of yin and yang, is clearly depicted in the Tai Qi symbol or what we commonly know as the yin-yang symbol.

Absolutely everything that exists in Creation ~ all life; all thought; all feeling and emotion; and everything in nature from the highest vibrations of light to the smallest manifestations of matter is birthed, sustained, and then resorbed in the continuous dance between the yin and yang expressions of Qi. These three movements of Qi are depicted in Vedic tradition as Brahma the Creator, Vishnu the Sustainer (balancer), and Shiva the Destroyer.

For Qi to execute her "gong", both characteristics of the relationship between the yin Qi and yang Qi are essential. The gong of Qi (its work, function, or purpose) is to reflect God, to bring forth God's image into the vibrational realities of Creation. But in order for the image of God's infinite beliefs and stories to appear as the infinite realities of Creation, the yin Qi and yang

Qi must be both dual in nature, separate from one another, and, at the same time, they must be one, united to each other in the balance formed from their complete

The gong of Qi, its work, function, or purpose, is to reflect God, to bring forth God's image into the vibrational realities of Creation.

giving and receiving of one another. This is the union of supreme balance between the yin and yang Qi, orchestrated by the Divine Intelligence of God Our Mother.

Qi is a vibrational entity, sustaining her place in and as Creation through the continuous and balanced exchange of force between the yin and yang. The yin Qi force and the yang Qi force are the two opposite poles or opposing characteristics of Qi expression ~ the yang Qi being the rising, expanding, repelling, and heating pole and the yin Qi being the sinking, contracting, attracting, and cooling pole. As energy, this dual nature of Qi expresses as a wave. In matter it is the tension between positively charged protons and negatively charged electrons. In the Causal (Mental) and Astral (Emotional) levels of our being, this dance manifests as the opposing sides of our every experience of thought, feeling, and emotion (see the Dualities of our Altars, ch. 15, pp, 227, 229, 231).

In the inorganic world, these forces and The Divine Intelligence orchestrating their balance permit the existence of everything in the firmament of Heaven ~ the galaxies, solar systems, planetary-moon systems, and all the compounds, molecules, and atoms within them. In the organic arena, yang Qi expresses as birth and growth, and yin Qi expresses as dissolution and death. In the balance of these forces is the miracle of life and the reproduction of life. This miracle is an intricate balance occurring in thousands of interconnected systems. The intelligence expressing through all of these systems is again our omniscient, omnipresent, omnipotent Mother orchestrating these many different interactions of yin and yang. These systems exists within each life form, governing the interplay between species, and the interplay between the organic and inorganic worlds.

This is how we now experience the dance between the opposing characteristics of Qi. But in this present time, our ability to perceive the entirety of Qi expression is limited, for there is a bigger picture, and we are presently only seeing the day-side half of it, and not the night-side half. We experience the yang characteristics of Qi as the Qi is entering the day-side of its expression, and we experience the yin characteristics of Qi as the Qi is leaving the day-side, moving toward its night-side expression. In other words, we are now only aware of the Qi in it expression between dawn and dusk, and have yet to know the night side expression of Qi.

So, in the big picture, the vibrational quality of Qi arises from its balanced movement, or cycling from its day-side, yang expression, to its night-side, yin expression, and back again, eternally. The epitome of the yang, as we presently experience it in nature, is the stars or suns of the galaxies. The epitome of the yin is the black holes of space that, relatively speaking, have only recently come into our awareness.

In Qi Gong Practice, we consciously invite God Our Mother, Qi, to participate in every part of our life for she is the Divine Medium in which we experience God. Through God Our Mother, we receive the keys that again open us to trust and allow her to form the union of supreme balance, the vibrational expression of God's Oneness and Love. And through her, we are guided and helped in surrendering our consciousness, and who we have believed we are, to this Oneness.

Who We Are

We are the union of Qi, our Mother, and Spirit, our Father. Through the act of creation, our Mother has given all of herself to us. Through her, we embody the entirety of Creation ~ all the energy, matter, and intelligence of Creation and all the expressions of life within her.

With our Father, on the other hand, comes the huge mystery of time immemorial, for he too has given all of himself to us. The One Spirit of God, who is beyond Creation, beyond all thought and feeling and beyond time, space, energy, and matter, is also Who We Are.

Our Mother also comes forth from the One Spirit of God. Hence, all of Creation, including our own created aspects, has ultimately come from the One Source. Our Father has given us both his Spirit and, by way of our Mother, our body as well, formed from all of her. The underlying truth then of Who We Are ~ we are God!

So, through the combined love of God and Creation, the trinity of Christ comes into being. The Oneness and Love of God as the One Spirit, and the Oneness and Love of God Our Mother as Creation, are shared completely in the creation of the Christ Child. The triune expression of Christ is all life, culminating in the awakened consciousness of Oneness and Love.

The union of all that God is, and all that Creation is, forms the individualized Soul, body, and consciousness of Christ. Each human being is a Christ Being. We are the One Spirit of God (Soul, Our Father) clothed in the reflection of the One Spirit of God (body, Our Mother), manifesting as the living experiencer of both of them (Christ Consciousness, the child). We are simply God, clothed in God, experiencing God.

As you already know, for it is part of Christ's gifts, we are the fulfillment of God and Creation's love. We are the faculty of God to experience Creation and the faculty of Creation to experience God. The miracle of Christ is that through our experience of Creation, God consciously experiences the Oneness and Love he gives to Creation and receives from her, and Creation, too, consciously experiences the Oneness and Love she gives to God and receives from him. In our experience of Creation is God and Creation's gifting to one another, their mutual expressions of gratitude, and the sharing of themselves

The union of all that God is, and all that Creation is, forms the individualized Soul, body, and consciousness of Christ. Each human being is a Christ Being.

with each other. We, as Christ, form the two-way bridge of giving and receiving that consummates their marriage.

God is love, but through Christ, love now becomes God, Creation and Christ's sharing of themselves completely with one another. Christ Consciousness is the living experience of giving all of oneself and receiving all of oneself, for in the living wisdom of Christ, there is only one Spirit, and all that exists is one in this Spirit. In this wisdom, it is known that everything that one gives is what one receives. Giving and receiving are one action.

This quality of giving and receiving is the holiness of Christ:
- It is God giving all of itself and receiving all of itself
- It is the act of Creating, then experiencing Creation
- It is the One Spirit of God giving itself unto Creation and unto us, and Creation and we returning ourselves unto God
- It is the knowing that all existence is oneself and that all actions are to oneself

This holy wisdom is love, the force binding God, Creation, and Christ in oneness.

In the giving of all of Who We Are, we receive all of Who We Are. We are, and have always been, Oneness and Love. We are this holy quality of giving and receiving. This is the true path to our resurrection.

We Have Forgotten

Each one of us chose to extend our self into Creation. Each of us has become an individualized expression of the one, infinite Spirit, clothed in a sacred body given to us and formed from our Mother. As we have descended into the vibrational realms of Creation, we have lost our way. We have directed our awareness primarily into Creation through a system of beliefs founded on a falsity or incomplete truth ~ that there exists a power that opposes God.

Why we have chosen to hold on to this belief as our truth, I cannot say. What I do know is that this belief is a piece of the infinity of God, and that we can choose to not hold on to this belief as easily as hold on to it (many spiritual traditions hold that this "why", and for that matter any *why question*, is unanswerable).

This belief and our choice to believe in it has permitted us to experience a reflection of God, a reality within Creation, in which everything that exists is separate from everything else and each thing that exists, including our own being, is formed from opposing forces or sides. Our holding on to this belief as our truth has caused us to experience everything as a duality ~ every thought, feeling, emotion, and perception of energy and matter.

We bind our consciousness to this interplay between the yin and yang forces and the yin and yang sides that form our experiences by investing ourselves in what we believe to be, and therefore experience to be, the correct and purposeful side of our experiences. We also invest ourselves through repressing and even actively fighting against what we believe to be the wrong and useless side. We literally believe that through this judging and our subsequent actions arising from it, we will find or earn our way back to God and heaven. What we are not seeing here is that when we invest ourselves in one half of any experience, we make the other half equally real. And the end result is that we tether our consciousness to the ongoing experience of both.

This is the story of "The Fall of Man" ~ our having to leave the paradise garden, the truth of Who We Are, because we choose to eat of the Tree of Knowledge of Good and Evil; we choose to believe that Who We Are comes from the dualities of Creation and our judgements of them.

We fell further into the forgetting of Who We Are (the loss of what I call "our precious balance", ch. 5 pp 59-61), and therefore bound our consciousness to this reality even more, through our choice to believe that our identity and value come not from God, the One Source, but from our experiences of Creation. Through these beliefs and our experiences of their reflections, we have replaced our Core Truth (that we are the Oneness and Love of God) with these beliefs:

We are separate ~ Separate from God, Creation, and each other, and even separated within our own being.

We are limited ~ Limited in our knowledge, happiness, and power to manifest our will.

In these beliefs is also the belief that we cannot share ourselves completely because in our sense of being separate from all, and limited in all that we are and have, we believe that to share ourselves completely would mean loss, suffering, and death.

Knowing on every level of our being that we are Oneness and Love is the key to our limitless interconnection to Creation and our limitless power to live within her. As we have lost our sense of Oneness and Love, we have also lost our conscious connection to the Divine Intelligence and Power of God Our Mother. We no longer commune with her in the orchestration of Creation and the coordination of the forces of yin and yang. Not sensing the power of love uniting yin and yang and our oneness with this power, we have lost our trust in Creation.

We experience the power of nature, and yet, we believe that we are not connected to her. We believe that we are limited in our ability to live harmoniously and richly with her. We accept that without nature we would perish, and yet, at the same time believe that she, too, is limited in her ability to sustain us and supply our needs. In these beliefs, we experience nature through the intention of using her for our purposes. We have since sought to dominate Creation, to own

Though we have misplaced our deepest core truth and substituted other "truths" for it, we continue to be God, and the Christ Consciousness of God.

her, divide her, judge her parts as more and less important, and manipulate her accordingly.

Absolutely everything we are experiencing, everything that is real to us; our sense of identity, value, and purpose; the meanings we give to the people, things, and events of life; and the deep motives driving our thoughts, feelings, emotions, attitudes, and behaviors, is a belief we are choosing to bring before the mirror of Creation. And it is who we believe we are that guides us in these choices.

Though we have misplaced our deepest core truth and substituted other "truths" for it, we continue to be God, and the Christ Consciousness of God. This cannot change. Even what we are experiencing now continues to be the reflections of our God Self, our Soul. But the beliefs we are presently choosing to hold as our truth are only small pieces of us. They are not carrying the totality of God or the complete truth of our unlimited power.

For a very long time now, some traditions say for more than 13,000 years, we have not experienced life through the Consciousness of Oneness and Love. We have forgotten our deepest core truth; we have forgotten that we are Christ. The Consciousness of Oneness and Love, Christ Consciousness, has become but a dream to us as we have come to experience life through duality consciousness. Through this consciousness, we have identified with the beliefs of separation and limitation.

God has given us Oneness and Love and the inherent quality of God's Oneness and Love is infinite potential. We are the infinite potential of God. Within us are infinite beliefs and stories and therefore infinite possible experiences. Whatever we choose to hold as our truth is reflected back to us in the Qi of Creation to be our experience, to be our reality.

We just have forgotten the beliefs and stories of Oneness and Love. In our forgetting we have chosen to believe that we are separate from God, Creation, one another, and all the life forms and things around us. And we have chosen to believe that we are limited in what we can do, have, and give. Our present experience of Creation, of our brothers and sisters, and of our own selves, is a distorted image of God. It is only a very small piece of the Oneness and Love that we are!

IT IS SIMPLE. THERE IS only one thing choosing to express in three ways. We have given this one thing many names: God, Creator, Father, Spirit, Soul, and Consciousness of Oneness and Love. But it really comes down to oneness. The three expressions of this oneness are: The One Spirit, Creation, and Consciousness.

As I cast my story dust out over this oneness, a picture appears showing three, interconnecting trinities. The picture is of a plant giving forth two flowers, each flower being of two petals. Around each flower an aura of three layers has formed.

The whole plant including its two flowers is the One Spirit within which exist the flower of God's Creation and the flower of God's Consciousness. This is the trinity of God.

The flower of Creation is God Our Mother, the Divine

Intelligence overseeing and orchestrating the workings of all Creation. Within her the eternal dance of balance takes place between the forces of yin Qi and yang Qi. This is the trinity of Creation.

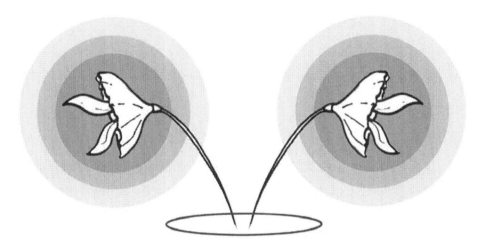

The flower of consciousness is Christ. We are the Christ Consciousness conceived in the holy union of our Soul (God) and our body (Creation). This is the trinity of Christ Consciousness.

The auras around each flower are trinities of a different kind. They are the envelopes of Qi that form the three vibrational bodies of Christ (mental, emotional, and energetic) and the three vibrational realms or planes of Creation (Causal, Astral, and Etheric). Our three bodies are intimately linked to the three realms of Creation, and it is through these links that our consciousness experiences Creation. About this I will soon speak much more. Let it suffice for now to say that the way our consciousness experienes Creation through these links directly affects everything: our relationship to God, Creation, and each other, who we believe we are, the quality of our life, and our reawakening. It is here, in the way our consciousness experiences the Qi, that Qi Gong Practice focuses and applies the Keys for the Transformation of Human Consciousness.

The trinity of God is a straightforward pattern showing that within the infinity of the One Spirit of God exists all Creation and all Consciousness. But as we focus on the two distinct trinities of Consciousness and Creation within the One Spirit, we see that their patterns have two directions:

- A creative direction of *one-becoming-three* indicates how the One Spirit divides itself into three aspects as it extends itself into Creation, and into Consciousness.
- A transcending or returning direction of *three-becoming-one* indicates how the three aspects of Creation or the three aspects of Consciousness can unite, transcending their separation to return into the One Spirit.

In the Trinity of Creation, the creative, *one-becoming-three* pattern shows the One Spirit of God extending itself as the Divine Intelligence of God Our Mother and the two forces of yin Qi and yang Qi expressing within her. But it is in the transcendent, *three-becoming-one* pattern that the purpose of Creation in the divine plan of God is revealed. The Divine Intelligence of God Our Mother, working through the yin Qi and yang Qi, forms a supreme balance between these forces. In this balance brought about by the inherent oneness of these forces, the manifesting image of God's infinite potential appears as the infinite realities of Creation.

In the Trinity of Consciousness, the creative, *one-becoming-three* pattern shows how the One Spirit of God extends an individual ray of itself as a Soul, and then encloses this Soul within a multilayered body formed from the Qi of Creation. In this sacred union of our Soul and body, our consciousness, the Consciousness of Christ, comes into being.

Now as we look at the transcendent, *three-becoming-one* pattern as it refers to the trinity of Christ Consciousness, we are witnessing nothing less than our reawakening, our transcendence of the separation we have experienced from God, Creation, and one another.

In the experience of our transcendence, we consciously accept and realize the precious balance of Who We Are. We, the Consciousness of Christ, are created in the balanced union of our Soul and body. What makes this balance so very precious is our knowing that our Soul is God while at the same time knowing that Creation, the source of our body, also is God. In our full acceptance and realization that we come solely from God, we access our Spiritual Body. Our transcendence is our conscious experience of our Soul reflected in our Spiritual Body. Through this experience, we consciously are the Oneness of God, Creation and Consciousness. This is the Core Event of Qi Gong Practice.

WHAT WE HAVE LEARNED UP to this point in the story is that Christ is the child of God and Creation. God gives all of itself to Christ, and Creation gives all of herself to Christ. Christ therefore is the Oneness and Love of both God and Creation. And Christ is the infinite potential of God, infinite beliefs and stories, and the infinite realities of Creation, the manifesting reflection of God's potential. All of this forms the individualized Soul and body of Christ. And we must not forget that each one of us is this Christ Being.

We have also learned that with the creation of Christ comes the most precious gifts: *conscious experience, the creation of life, the transformation of love, and Christ's unlimited power to bring into conscious experience any and all of the infinite potential within God.*

God extends itself as a Soul, a ray of Spirit, and Creation

encloses this Soul within her matter, energy, and intelligence. This embodiment of God by Creation forms the Christ Being. Christ is the individualization of God. Individualization brings Christ into the continuum of Creation, giving Christ a place within Creation from which to consciously experience, interrelate, and interact with Creation. Individualization allows the Soul of Christ to experience its reflection not only in Creation, but also in the body surrounding the Soul. The ability of Christ's Soul to experience this more intimate reflection plays an important part in the Consciousness of Christ.

> *The embodiment of God by Creation forms the Christ Being .... The spherical design of Christ permits the Soul to reflect itself in a body, and also forms the basis for all life.*

The design of the Christ being is a sphere. The sphere itself (our body) is a semi permeable, energetic membrane of Qi that places the infinity of God within Christ (our Soul) and the infinity of Creation without (the Qi of Creation reflecting both God and our Soul).

The spherical membrane around Soul is also a reflection of our Soul, albeit a more intimate reflection, and forms the spiritual, mental, emotional, energetic, and physical layers of our body.

The spherical design of Christ not only permits the Soul to reflect itself in a body, but also forms the basis for all life. Life comes into being in the balance of the inward and outward exchange of energy across this semi permeable, energetic membrane. The culmination of all life is the living temple that sustains the Consciousness of Oneness and Love, the Consciousness of Christ.

We know that we humans are Christ, though I believe that it is naïve to think that we are the only forms of life that carry Christ Consciousness. Of the life forms we know of, whales and dolphins are likely candidates as our brothers and sisters in Christ. I sense that there are other life forms we are not aware of that also are the vessels of this Consciousness.

The enclosing of God's Soul within a spherical body of Qi brings a most holy Consciousness into being. This most holy Consciousness is the essence of Christ; it is the essence of Who We Are. All of the gifts of Christ come out of this Consciousness.

The Consciousness of Christ is two fold: it is the Consciousness of Conscious Experience, and it is the Conscious Experience of Being Consciousness.

Consciousness of Conscious Experience

The Consciousness of Conscious Experience is the faculty of being conscious or aware of something relative to being conscious or aware of oneself. This consciousness is made possible because of the Soul's ability to experience its reflection in the Qi of its own body. Christ's Soul is reflected on the inside of his or her body of Qi while simultaneously being reflected by the Qi of all Creation.

It is in the relativity of these two events ~ the Soul's experience of its reflection from the inside of itself (the experience of self) relative to the Soul's experience of its reflection from the outside of itself (the experience of other than self), that the Consciousness of Conscious Experience arises.

Our ability to consciously experience Creation, a brother or sister, our body, and even our ability to experience that we are our Soul, depends on there being an experiencer.

The design of Christ's being gives rise to the Christ Consciousness of Conscious Experience. Within this consciousness the "I Am" or "Self" of Christ comes into existence as the experiencer. The "I Am" or "Self" of Christ is the sine qua non of conscious experience. Without it conscious experience cannot happen. It is the living "I Am" of Christ who consciously experiences Creation. It is also this living "I Am" who, through the Conscious Experience of Being Consciousness, experiences him or herself as being Soul, or the Oneness of God.

Through the Christ Consciouness of Conscious Experience, the Christ being experiences the reflection of God and the reflection of his or her Soul in Creation and in the mental, emotional, energetic, and physical layers of the body. The experiences of these internal reflections are Christ's thoughts, feelings and perceptions of his or her energetic and physical bodies.

What Christ experiences within his or her body and without, is the remembrance of who he or she is and the unique, individual role he or she has chosen to live. Christ also experiences the reflection of any beliefs he or she chooses to hold. We must remember that within God is infinite potential, infinite beliefs and stories, and Christ is the unlimited power to bring into conscious experience any and all of the infinite potential within God.

The primary role of Christ is to sustain his or her conscious connection to God, the one source of all Creation and all life. But, moreover, the role of Christ is to translate this conscious connection into a living wisdom. This wisdom is the natural way of a living Christ who consciously experiences and expresses the beliefs of Oneness and Love within Creation.

The Christ Consciousness of Conscious Experience places Christ into Creation as a living being. It permits Christ to consciously experience, interrelate, and interact with the infinite potentials of God as the manifesting realities of Creation. One of the precious gifts of Christ is Christ's unlimited power to bring into conscious experience any and all of God's infinite potential. With this power also comes the power of discernment, the power to choose which of the infinite beliefs and stories of God are to be consciously experienced as real. What guides Christ's discernment is Christ's wisdom. Christ is continually learning through his or her individually, unique experience of God, and is continually adding to the collective wisdom of all Christ Beings.

The Conscious Experience of Being Consciousness

As a Christ Being, each one of us sustains our connection to God by consciously experiencing our Soul. Our Soul is God. It is eternally reminding us that we are God, that we are Oneness and Love. Our Soul also is the access to the collective wisdom of all Christ Beings; it is the source of our guidance and help. We experience our Soul through three pathways:

- We experience the reflection of our Soul in the Qi of Creation and in the Qi of our sisters and brothers.
- We experience the reflection of our Soul in the mental, emotional, energetic, and physical Qi of our body.
- And we have the ability to experience our Soul directly by focusing our awareness inward toward the Soul.

All three pathways open us into the ultimate experience

of Christ Consciousness ~ the Conscious Experience of Being Consciousness. This most holy Consciousness is the continuing revelation that we are God. This Consciousness is our remembrance.

In the Conscious Experience of Being Consciousness, we are experiencing our Soul reflected in our Spiritual Body. Our Spiritual Body is always revealing our connection to God. Our Spiritual Body is still a form of Qi, albeit a Qi of such subtle nature and in such supreme balance that Qi and consciousness become one. In this conscious experience of our Soul, we transcend all duality. We as the experiencer are one with the experienced, while at the same time holding all other experiences of consciousness.

This living experience of being consciousness is our natural state of being. In this state of being, we live, experience, and express Oneness and Love. We know that there is one Spirit, and all that exists is one in this Spirit. And we know that we are love, that in giving ourselves openly and authentically, we receive ourselves eternally.

By living this wisdom, the balance of our being is the balance in the yin and yang Qi of Creation and the balance in the Qi of our thoughts, feelings, and body. In our balance, we experience the undistorted image of God within ourselves and without. We perceive our true reflection.

42

In being this living consciousness, we are the open door,
the eternal invitation to all
Creation and all life to know
and live the Oneness and
Love that we all share with
God.

*In the Conscious Experience
of Being Consciousness, we
are experiencing our Soul
reflected in our Spiritual
Body .... In this conscious
experience of our Soul, we
transcend all duality. We as
the experiencer are one with
the experienced.*

Talking about consciousness
itself; what it is, what it does, or how it works, is
much like talking about God. Where God or Spirit is
beyond concept, thought, feeling, energy, matter, time,
and space, and yet is the source of absolutely everything,
consciousness too, is beyond all of these things. And yet,
like God, consciousness touches absolutely everything
that exists.

We must remember that God is Oneness and Love, one
Spirit, and the complete giving or extension of that one
Spirit. Spirit becomes everything; there is nothing else.
Consciousness then is the way, the how, or the medium
by which Spirit extends itself throughout all Creation.
It is the mystical, omnipresent web of Oneness and Love
connecting God to all things, and connecting all things
to one another.

Consciousness is about relationship. It is about the
experiencing, interrelating, and interacting occurring
between Spirit, Christ, and Creation. It is the way our
Soul experiences, interrelates and interacts with the

Qi of Creation and with the Qi of our many-layered body. And consciousness is how everything that exists experiences, interrelates, and interacts with God, God Our Mother, Christ, and one another.

The quality or nature of how consciousness expresses is different in the different kingdoms of existence (i.e. the mineral, plant, and animal kingdoms) and also varies within a kingdom (i.e. a bacteria, snake or elephant all within the animal kingdom). Consciousness is not just one kind of experience or one kind of interrelating or interacting; it is a range of experiences as varied as Creation itself.

The spectrum of consciousness spans the entire inorganic kingdom, moves through all forms of life, reaching Christ Consciousness. In the inorganic kingdom, consciousness is the Divine Intelligence of God Our Mother. She is the omniscience, omnipotence, and omnipresence coordinating the balance in the yin and yang forces of Qi and orchestrating the workings of all Creation.

In the organic kingdoms, consciousness is Christ, for Christ is all life and the culmination of life. The Christ Consciousness of Conscious Experience encompasses the vast range of experiencing, interrelating, and interacting that occurs throughout all forms of life; from single cell organisms, through the ever-increasing complexity of multi-cellular life forms, to the divine temple of the human being.

WE HAVE COME TO SEE that within our being a most holy Consciousness comes into existence. This Consciousness is the Consciousness of God. As we are consciously experiencing Creation and one another, God is consciously experiencing through us. In our shared Consciousness, we also get to consciously experience the Oneness and Love of God.

As a Christ being, we play many roles, but the overarching theme of our existence is to experience. We have come here to experience the unfathomable wonder of God, and to experience the indescribable joy of being this wonder.

Though we all come into this life to experience, we each do it in our own way. Each one of us is an individually unique expression of God, choosing our own unique experiences. What we each discover becomes our wisdom, a wisdom that, in love, we openly and authentically share with all life and all Creation.

We have come here to experience the unfathomable wonder of God, and to experience the indescribable joy of being this wonder.

To Remember We Are Oneness

Foremost, our role is to sustain the open channel of conscious oneness that we are. We are the Christ Consciousness of Conscious Experience, the "I Am" that experiences, interrelates and interacts with all Creation, and the Christ Consciousness that consciously experiences being all consciousness. We are the mystical web uniting God, Creation, and all life. Our consciousness is the Consciousness of God.

This is our remembrance. We sustain our remembrance by living our remembrance. We allow our deep sense of Oneness and Love to motivate us in choosing our beliefs about Who We Are. We then translate these beliefs into our unique expression of God and our unique experience of reality. It is our remembrance that guides us; it is our eternal connection to God.

An important part of our remembrance is our sustaining the precious balance of our being. We are a most precious balance of God and Creation. It is in their union that our consciousness comes into being.

The essential key to our sustaining this balance is our remembering that Creation comes out of God. Creation is the reflection of God, and it is the reflection of our Soul. Spirit does not come from Creation. Our Soul does not come from Creation. We are one with all Creation, but our source, and the source of Creation, is God.

When we believe that our source is Creation, or that our value comes from Creation, or believe that we need anything from Creation to be whole, we begin to lose our precious balance, and we begin to forget Who We Are. Through the loss of our balance, we experience a distorted image of ourselves and Creation.

To know and live the individually unique role we have chosen, we must know ourselves. What we have come to this earth to experience and share, and how to accomplish it, is written in our Soul. As we direct our consciousness within, we sense in our Soul the unique abilities we have brought into this incarnation, and we sense the unfolding of the unique life path we have chosen to walk this time.

To Love

We are also love, and as Christ, we are the transformation of love. Love is the giving of all of oneself, the sharing of oneself openly and authentically. In the Love of Christ, we give all of ourselves, we share all of Who We Are with Creation and our brothers and sisters. In this giving, we receive all of ourselves. This is the wisdom of our love; this is the transformation of love in Christ. We are the living knowledge that there is only one Spirit and all that exists is one in this Spirit. All that we give, we give unto ourselves. In Christ, giving and receiving are one action.

Our expression of this Love is another important piece in our remembrance; it is our continual resurrection. In giving all of Who We Are, we receive all of Who We Are: We receive God, and we receive life eternal.

We sustain our conscious oneness with God, Creation, and one another by living our deep sense of God's Love through the following:

- *Absolute inclusion* ~ We accept every expression of life and aspect of Creation as being part of ourselves. We include everything.
- *Equality* ~ We approach each thing in reverence, sensing the sanctity and equal importance of each part of Creation.
- *Infinite potential* ~ We see the infinite potential of God in everything. We offer our help and guidance to every life form and piece of Creation in its evolution in consciousness.

Our love is the completion of God and Creation's Love. In our love, in sharing all of Who We Are openly and authentically with Creation and one another, we complete the circle through which God and Creation consciously experience and love each other. In our giving of ourselves, not only do we receive ourselves, but God and Creation, too, receive themselves.

Our primary role then is to remember Who We Are and to live our truth ~ to know, feel, be, experience, and express the Oneness and Love we share with God, Creation, and one another.

To Commune With God Our Mother

Another part of our role is to be in conscious communion with God Our Mother, the substance, power, and Divine Intelligence of Creation.

In our creation, God Our Mother gives all of herself to us. Her infinite body is our body and through this gift, our consciousness comes into existence. Her infinite power and intelligence also are our power and intelligence. In this shared oneness, we sit in council with God Our Mother in overseeing the workings of all Creation. We participate with her in holding the supreme balance in the forces of yin and yang.

The balance in the yin and yang forces of Creation is directly linked to our own balance. Our balance is the precious balance of our knowing and, therefore, being God and Creation. We sustain this balance by remembering that our source and Creation's source is God. Our balance is also our expression of love, the giving of all of Who We Are and receiving all of Who We Are.

Our remembrance is the key to our conscious connection to God Our Mother, and it is the key to our unlimited power to live freely and abundantly within her. It is in

Creation's balance that we experience the undistorted reflection of God and our Soul.

The balance we sustain in our own being is directly linked to the yin and yang Qi within God Our Mother.

The sacred design of our being is the design of life. Like us, every life form comes into being as the infusion of spirit into Creation. We are life, and our Christ Consciousness is the culmination of life. All life is moving through the sacred geometries formed in the energies and elements of Creation. Being the totality of this journey, we, as Christ, work cooperatively with God Our Mother in the creation of life, and in guiding and helping all life forms in their evolutionary journey to God.

To Learn and Share

Each one of us is continually learning through our unique experiences of our Soul, Creation, and one another. All that we learn we openly share, adding our wisdom to the collective wisdom of Christ.

Through the experience of our Soul, our deep sense of being Oneness and Love, we choose experiences and expressions for our life that teach us and help us to, even more, open the doors of Oneness and Love. This is part of our role, to learn the navigational system of Oneness and Love.

We are refining and expanding our belief system and the

collective belief system of Oneness and Love. Our choice of beliefs, what we choose to believe in and hold as sacred from the infinite beliefs and stories within God, is based on our own sense of being Oneness and Love, and our wisdom of what Oneness and Love is. We are eternally expanding both our sensing and our wisdom by consciously experiencing our choices in the mirror of Creation and our body.

Creation is the mirror. She is the Qi that reflects God's infinite potential. She is the infinite manifesting realities of God's infinite beliefs and stories. Creation unerringly responds to our will, giving us experiences of the realities that correspond to the beliefs and stories we choose.

In Christ Consciousness, in the Conscious Experience of Being Consciousness, we are fully open to our Soul. Our power to bring any and all of God's infinite potential into our conscious experience aligns with the will of God. Our will and God's will are one will. Our alignment, our opening to God, extends the liberating wisdom of Christ throughout Creation infinitely and eternally.

GOD, THROUGH LOVE, EXTENDS ITSELF as the entirety of Creation; Creation is the reflection of God.

God and Creation extend themselves to create Christ; Christ is the union of both God and Creation.

Christ, as an individual being, becomes the ability of God to consciously experience Creation. Through Christ, God is able to sense, feel, see, smell, hear and taste his holy reflection.

Creation is not only God's reflection, but Christ's reflection as well, for God is within Christ. Creation is the manifesting reflection of the infinite beliefs and potential stories within God, and Creation is also the manifesting reflection of the infinite beliefs and potential stories within Christ. And here is the crucial point ~ Christ is also the power to choose which beliefs and stories are experienced consciously.

We are Christ; it is you and I who decide which beliefs and stories will become our experiences of reality.

So how do we choose or form our beliefs? We choose or

Who we believe we are motivates our thoughts, feelings and attitudes. These become our outlook on life; our experience of reality, the way we engage the world, and our perception of ourselves and others.

form our beliefs from two sources: our sense of self, and our experience of the world. Both contribute to our choosing or forming the deep beliefs about Who We Are, the choosing or forming of our identity.

Who we believe we are motivates our thoughts, feelings and attitudes. These become our outlook on life; our experience of reality, the way we engage the world, and our perception of ourselves and others.

How we choose or form our beliefs, and thus, what we experience in the world, ultimately comes down to who we believe we are. A feedback loop then forms in which our most deeply held beliefs about Who We Are influences our experiences of the world. Our experiences of the world then come back to us to prove the validity of our beliefs and stories.

The question now becomes who do we believe we are? This question brings us to the core cause of our experiences. What I believe, what I understand Qi and the practice of Qi Gong to be saying, and what the story says, is that we are Christ. As a Christ Being, we are a precious balance of Spirit (God) and Creation, Creation being the reflection of Spirit and the giver of our holy body. Through this gift, we have individualization, and it is our individualization that gives rise to the gifts of Christ ~ *life, conscious experience, the transformation of love, and the power of choice.*

Being a Christ Being, being both Spirit and Creation, is a precious, and yet, tricky balance. Our deepest core truth is that we are Spirit; we are the Oneness and Love of God. And we are also Creation, but what we must remember is that Creation comes from Spirit. Creation is the reflection of Spirit, and therefore is our reflection too. Again, the deepest core truth is that there is only one thing, Spirit, and everything in Creation, including us, is this one thing.

The miracle of Christ is that Spirit can live within Creation as the Consciousness of Oneness and Love. This is Who We Are. We are the Consciousness of God, living within Creation, our reflection.

The sacred key to life and knowing how to live our unique, individual life is to remember Who We Are, and live this truth. We are God; our source is God. We are the Consciousness of Oneness and Love. As Oneness and Love, we give or extend all of ourselves, and therefore receive all of ourselves. This is our divine role, to be both the creator (Spirit) and the created (Creation), while remembering that all Creation, including our own manifesting aspect, comes from Spirit. Through this act, we live the truth of Who We Are; we experience the truth of being Spirit and Creation, and we sustain our conscious remembrance, the precious balance we embody.

We have forgotten Who We Are. We have chosen to believe that Creation is the source of Who We Are, and that our personal value or worth comes from Creation. Subsequently, we have lost the center in our precious balance of being Spirit and Creation, and we have forgotten how to live through love.

Creation is our reflection; we are one with her. She gives us our body, our individualization, and makes possible the beautiful gifts of Christ. But in our believing that we come from Creation, we begin to experience a distorted image of Creation and ourselves, for the mirror of Creation begins to reflect the subsequent beliefs that stem from this fundamental error.

As we lose the precious balance of knowing and living Who We Are, we lose the deep sense or feeling of being the expanding Consciousness of Oneness and Love. This deep sense or feeling is what guides us in our choosing the beliefs and stories we experience as reality. We then start down a pathway of contracting consciousness. This pathway leads into the feedback loop that cycles us further into beliefs of separation ~ separated inside of ourselves; separated from our true self; and separated from God, Creation, and each other, and beliefs of limitation ~ limited in our knowledge, happiness, and power to manifest our will; and limited in our ability to love.

The union of supreme balance in the yin and yang forces of Qi forms God's reflection and our reflection as well. It is in this balance that Creation comes into being; we exist, and conscious experience is possible. The Divine Intelligence of God Our Mother, the third power in the Trinity of Creation, coordinates the balance in the forces of yin and yang. Our balance is intimately linked to this supreme balance in the yin and yang Qi of Creation. We are one with God Our Mother. Her intelligence and power is our intelligence and power; the supreme balance in her forces of yin and yang is a reflection of our balance. Through our balance we commune with God Our Mother in balancing the forces of yin and yang and overseeing the workings of all Creation. The holy keys to our limitless interconnection to God and Creation and our limitless power is our remembrance of Who We Are, and living through love. This is how we sustain our balance.

In our forgetting, we have lost our conscious connection to the Divine Intelligence and power of Creation; we are no longer conscious of our sacred role in the holy relationship between Spirit, Creation and Christ. Our imbalance alters the supreme balance in the yin and yang forces of Qi, causing even more distortion in the holy reflection. We experience ourselves as separate from God, Creation and each other, and we experience ourselves as limited in our power to live freely in Creation and participate in her inner workings.

In our belief that we are lacking, that we are somehow not good enough, we judge Creation according to our perceived needs, and then seek to control and own her.

Cycling further into the beliefs of separation and limitation, our experience becomes even more distorted. We come to believe that we must get something from Creation and from our brothers and sisters to be whole and complete. Creation, of course, reflects this belief. It becomes not only part of the feedback loop that further distorts our experience, but now motivates us to manipulate Creation. In our belief that we are lacking, that we are somehow not good enough, we judge Creation according to our perceived needs, and then seek to control and own her. This drive to acquire our identity and our worth from Creation now becomes a conscious and blatant manipulation of the yin and yang Qi of Creation. No longer worshipping Creation as the reflection of God, no longer thanking her and working in harmony with her, we, in our myopic consciousness, now just take from her.

At this point, our awareness, our spiritual power, is directed almost exclusively outside of us. Here too, we have lost our balance, forgetting how to look within ourselves toward our Soul. We are not able to see the truth within us, that we are both God the unknowable (our Spirit) and Creation the knowable (our body and all that surrounds us) and that absolutely everything comes from our Spirit.

In our loss of balance, in our forgetting Who We Are, we have lost our conscious connection to our Soul; our sense of oneness, our sense of eternity, equality, balance, infinite potential for all, and love (the complete giving of ourselves openly and authentically). Therefore, we have lost our internal guidance in choosing the beliefs and stories that are Who We Are, the beliefs and stories that are the source of the realities of Oneness and Love and the source of unlimited power that is ours through love.

OUR PATH IS THE CONTINUING revelation of Who We Are;
it is the path of God realization, the path of eternal life.
As we walk this path, we are translating into a living
experience the truth we choose to hold as our own. In the
attunement of our beliefs with the Consciousness of God,
we are the living expression of love and consciously express
the unlimited power of God on this earth and in all Creation.

And yet, we have chosen to attach or harmonize our
consciousness to a system of beliefs that vibrate outside
of the spectrum of Oneness and Love. Subsequently,
our consciousness has fallen out of attunement to the
Consciousness of God. We have forgotten Who We Are.
We have lost sight of our path and how to walk this
path. What we are now experiencing and expressing is a
distorted image of God and ourselves.

These three questions:

- Who am I?
- What is my role in this life?
- How am I to live this role?

Our Consciousness is the holder of who we believe we are. As our system of belief aligns to Oneness and Love, our consciousness harmonizes with the consciousness of God.

are the guideposts marking the path we walk as a Christ Being. In this treatise, we have been on an exploration into these questions. Along the way, it has become clear that the answers are all rooted in the answer to the first question, "Who am I?" Consciously asking "Who am I?" and consciously living the answers we discover is our primary role in this life (and the answer to the second question). This also is the primary intention in the practice of Qi Gong. The answer to the third question "How are we to live this role?" also is revealed to us in our conscious exploration of Who We Are. The "how" is the guidance and help extended to us by God, Creation, and Christ as we walk the inner path. This guidance and help is the real power and gift of Qi Gong Practice.

The answers to these questions come from our Soul. Our Soul is God. When we ask these questions, we receive the answers in our consciousness, either directly from our Soul or through our experience of our Soul's reflection coming from Creation and our body. Our Soul always responds to our questions through these three pathways.

In the Consciousness of Conscious Experience, we experience the answers coming to us from Creation or coming to us through our body as our thoughts, feelings, and our energetic and physical sensations and movements. As we consciously experience that we are consciousness (the Conscious Experience of Being Consciousness), we experience the reflection of our Soul in our Spiritual Body. In this consciousness, we come to know that we are the answer to all questions.

Our answers to these three questions are our experience of life. In consciously asking these questions, we are consciously participating in the evolution of our beliefs; we are consciously changing our expression of consciousness and our experience of life and self. This is the practice of Qi Gong.

Being Christ, we encompass all expressions of consciousness. The expression of consciousness through which we experience, interrelate, and interact is directly linked to the beliefs we choose to hold as our truth. Our consciousness is the holder of who we believe we are. As our system of belief aligns to Oneness and Love, our consciousness harmonizes with the Consciousness of God. Our experience of Creation and our experience of our body and Soul expand toward oneness. Our role in this life and how we accomplish this role also then expands.

The only thing that separates us from being and expressing the unlimited love, wisdom, joy, and power of our Soul is our attachment to beliefs that stand outside of the vibration of Oneness and Love. It is here that we catch a glimpse of the Essence Movement of Qi Gong Practice: the release of our attachment to everything that separates us from our Soul. Within the wisdom of Qi Gong Practice

The only thing that separates us from being and expressing the unlimited love, wisdom, joy, and power of our Soul is our attachment to beliefs that stand outside of the vibration of Oneness and Love.

are the transformational keys that guide and help us in this releasing.

Qi Gong Practice is the natural path of Christ. It is what we naturally do to not forget Who We Are and to translate Who We Are into a living reality. The practice of Qi Gong can also be a path of reawakening, a way back to our conscious oneness with our Soul and Creation when it has been forgotten. In this way, the power and wisdom in the practice is similar to how eating well, exercising, and getting plenty of rest are essential practices for staying healthy. At the same time, these same practices can restore health when we have fallen ill. In this time, Qi Gong Practice has become this path, a way by which we return to Who We Are, the Consciousness of Oneness and Love uniting us with God, Creation, and one another.

Three Sacred Principles

We are presently in the time of a transformation of human consciousness in which we are rediscovering the oneness we share with God and all Creation. It is therefore from this perspective of rediscovery that the theory and the method of Qi Gong Practice will be shared.

Qi Gong Practice is the conscious path of human life. It is a wisdom that has guided and helped human beings from the beginning to both sustain our oneness with God and Creation and to rediscover this oneness when it has been forgotten. Always, the intention in Qi Gong Practice is to share completely with all human beings the truth of Who We Are, both as a collective and individually, and to help us understand and apply the natural principles of God's Love. These principles govern Creation and consciousness and govern our relationship, as the Consciousness of Christ, with God and Creation.

Qi Gong Practice is the language of our oneness. It is a conversation continually taking place in our physical, energetic, emotional, mental, and spiritual levels of being. It is the language by which our Soul, our consciousness, and the Qi of our body and Creation, consciously commune.

Qi Gong Practice is spirituality. The practice is about the One Spirit of God and how all Creation, all consciousness, and all life come from this One Spirit, and in truth are all one in this Spirit. This truth is also the foundation of love, the open and authentic sharing of all of oneself. God's Oneness and Love sets the precedent for all the natural principles governing Creation, consciousness, and life.

It is through God's Oneness and the complete extension of God through love that all Creation comes into existence and is eternally sustained. And it is through God and Creation's Oneness and the complete extension of them both through love that we, the Consciousness of Christ, come into being.

In receiving all of God and all of Creation, we have also been given the sacred principles of love. These are the principles of our oneness with God, Creation, and one another, and these are the principles by which the infinite power of God and Creation is channeled through our being.

Let me share three of these principles:

- Though Creation and each of us is God, both Creation and we are created by God and in eternal service to our Creator.
- Though Creation and each one of us come from God, you and I do not come from Creation.
- The Consciousness of Christ that we are is the ultimate Consciousness of God. Being this Consciousness, we are the ability to consciously experience the totality of Creation, but we do not come from these experiences. We are not limited or confined by our experiences of Creation, nor do our experiences of Creation have power over us.

Quite the contrary, we choose our experiences. This

power to choose our experiences is but one expression of the limitless power given to us by God.

These principles are essential to the practice of Qi Gong and our remembrance of Who We Are. Creation and our body, as part of Creation, reflect to us Who We Are and who we believe we are, but our identity and worth come only from God. In this way, the Qi is our great teacher, for she is always showing us God and our beliefs about our relationship with God and Creation. All of our experiences are always leading us to God and Love.

THE SECOND PART
of the
THREE PART STORY

How I Forgot

WITHIN EACH OF US

Chapter Seven

The Core Event

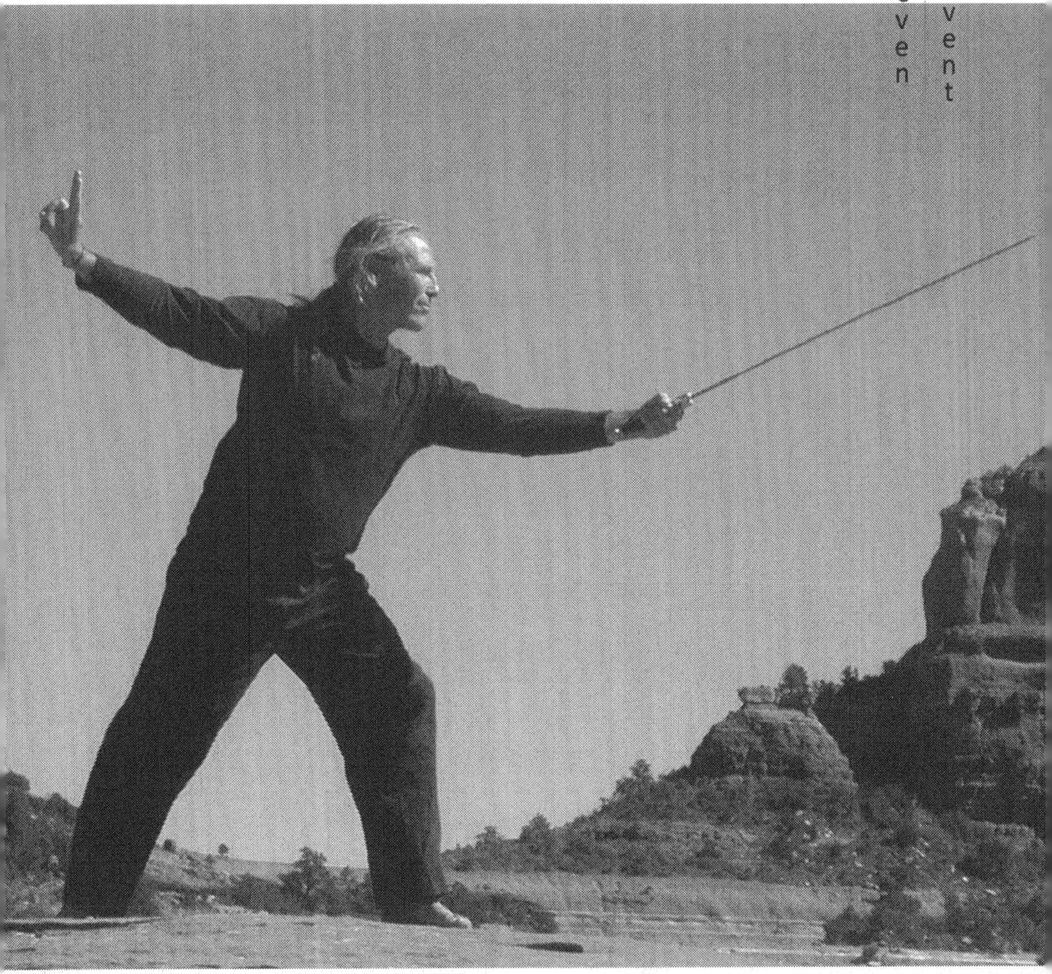

THE CORE EVENT OF QI GONG PRACTICE is our conscious experience of the one absolute truth. It is our conscious experience of heaven on earth. It is our conscious experience of being God.

I do not believe that this event is our final initiation into the one truth. It is what I have said it is ~ our conscious experience of being God and our ability, as Christ, to consciously experience God in all Creation. I do believe that each one of us as the Christ Being and Consciousness will transcend consciousness and Qi altogether. That passage, which will be our entrance into heaven, is beyond the scope of this book, and is the primary difference between this body of work and the message shared with us through The Course In Miracles. The focus of this book is the return of Christ to this earth, which is happening now in the time we are living in.

Through the principle of God's Love, God has given all of itself to us. We are the Oneness and Love of God unifying these three expressions of God (ch. 8, pp 94-96):

When we chose to hold as our truth that there exists a power that opposes God, we separated within ourselves and began to experience a divided and limited world outside of ourselves as well.

- The One Spirit of God is our Soul.
- The whole of Creation is our body; which we now know through the remembrance of our precious balance, comes from God.
- Christ, the holy child conceived in the union of our Soul and body, is the Consciousness of God and our Christ Consciousness.

The Consciousness of Christ is the essence of Who We Are now. As the fully awake Christ, we consciously experience ourselves as being the Oneness and Love from which everything comes and in which everything exists. Being Christ, we are the whole spectrum of consciousness, every level of consciousness, able to travel freely in and consciously experience every expression of God, while simultaneously being the unifying Oneness and Love of everything (God).

We are and have always been the Oneness and Love of God. Our conscious return into being the Consciousness of Oneness and Love is the return of Christ. This reawakening is the ***Core Event of Qi Gong Practice***.

Designed by the Divine Intelligence of God Our Mother

and built out of the three vibrational levels of her Qi, our being is God's temple. The Central Altar of this temple is God's heart and is also our Sacred Heart. This altar is the well spring from which all Creation, all consciousness, and all life flows, and it is the passage of transcendence by which all the expressions of God can return to the Oneness of God. It is through this altar that God consciously experiences all of its Creation, and it is the holy meeting place where God, God Our Mother, and Christ commune.

The Core Event of Qi Gong Practice occurs within our temple when we, as the Consciousness of Christ, stand before this most holy altar.

When we chose to hold as our truth that there exists a power that opposes God, we separated within ourselves and began to experience a divided and limited world outside of ourselves as well. At that time, our Central Altar and Spiritual Body became the three sacred altars, or tan tiens, of our being and the mental, emotional and energetic layers of our body (our physical body exists within our energy body). It is through these three distinct altars that we presently experience a version of Creation formed from three distinct vibrational realms: the Causal, Astral, and Etheric realms.

As you will soon understand (ch. 13 pp 208-209, ch. 15 pp 222-223), these three altars can only stay separated from each other for as long as there

82

continues to exist an unbalance in the yin and yang Qi that forms and maintains them. The healing of this unbalance within each of these altars is what the Essence Movement of Qi Gong Practice is all about.

Since Qi is also the Oneness and Love of God, she is always seeking to express oneness. The Oneness and Love of God manifest within her as the union of supreme balance that she orchestrates between the yin forces and yang forces of Qi. This balance naturally forms within each altar and each realm of Creation when we, as consciousness, allow the yin Qi forces and yang Qi forces to flow into each other. How we allow this supreme balance to occur within our three altars is one of the main focuses of this book. Trusting and allowing the Qi to form this balance and the surrender of ourselves (and all that we have believed we are) into this balance is the Essence Movement of Qi Gong Practice.

Once the union of supreme balance is reestablished within each of our three sacred altars, the stage is set for the real magic to happen. Because they are formed from Qi, each of our altars vibrates and each altar has its own, distinct vibrational rate. In this sense, our altars are like tones in a musical scale. Through Creation's laws of harmonics, the vibrational tones of our altars are actually three expressions or pieces of a oneness. This plays out in music when we see how three tones in a musical scale can harmonize with one another to form a chord ~ when three come together as one. The oneness that forms within us, as our three sacred altars harmonize, is our Central Altar or Spiritual Body.

This Holy of Holies has been given many names: Central Altar, Spiritual Body, Sacred Heart, Heart of God, Place of Meeting. But in the end, this altar is the spiritualized Qi that, upon receiving God and our Soul, reflects them into vibrational existence, into Creation, perfectly.

In the Core Event, we, as consciousness, stand before this altar and consciously experience the pure reflection of our Soul. In this experience, we again recognize that we are the actualized Christ. We consciously experience being and having always been God, Creation, and Christ, and the ultimate Oneness and Love unifying them all.

The Core Event of Qi Gong Practice, where the practice is leading us, is our return to this ultimate Consciousness of God, the Consciousness of Oneness and Love. This core event is what I like to refer to as "The Meeting", for when we participate in Qi Gong Practice we are bringing together all the expressions of God; we are consciously inviting them into oneness. As a living Christ, we are both the facilitator of this meeting, and we are the very temples in which this meeting takes place. But in order for us to host this meeting, we have to remember Who We Are.

We are the Consciousness of Christ, conceived in the holy union of God and Creation. In our creation, we have been given many gifts. One of these is the Consciousness of Conscious Experience (ch. 3, pp 39-41), the ability to consciously experience God, Creation, and ourselves. Because of Who We Are, we openly share this gift with God and Creation. In us, God, Creation, and we, the

In the Core Event, we, as consciousness, stand before our Central Altar and consciously experience the pure reflection of our Soul. ...This event is our conscious experience of being the ultimate consciousness of God when Spirit, Qi, and consciousness are one.

Consciousness of Christ, consciously experience each other. Our ability to consciously experience now is their ability to consciously experience. And so it is that we are the living temple in which this meeting takes place, for it is in our being that the three expressions of God; the One Spirit, Creation, and Consciousness, come into conscious communion as our Soul, body, and consciousness.

Another gift is our power to choose. We, as Christ, are the unlimited power to choose which beliefs, from the infinite beliefs and stories within God, will be reflected in the Qi of Creation to become our reality. And so it is that we are the facilitators of this meeting. We, through power of choice, invite this meeting into our conscious experience and into our vibrational reality.

This meeting is the Core Event of Qi Gong Practice ~ the transcendence of our separation from God, Creation and one another. In this Core Event, we consciously experience the pure reflection of our God Self (our

Soul) in our Spiritual Body. This event is our conscious experience of being the ultimate Consciousness of God when Spirit, Qi, and consciousness are one.

This meeting is also the spiritual council of the highest order in which God, God Our Mother, and we, as Christ, join together in the continuous creation of all existence and all life. And finally, this Core Event is the Heart of God. It is here that the infinite mind and the infinite body of God are eternally joined; Christ is this eternal union.

The Core Event is the natural state of relationship existing between God, Creation, and the Consciousness of Christ; it is the harmony naturally arising out of our shared Oneness and Love. So how do we allow this natural event, this "meeting" to take place within us? Our ability to participate in this meeting and our way into this harmony is our own vibration of Oneness and Love. The vibration of Oneness and Love is the sacred key by which we return to God. We must discover the Oneness and Love that exists within us, the Oneness and Love we have always been, the same Oneness and Love extended to us from God.

This is the answer to the third question, "How am I to live my role?" The path of our reawakening to the oneness we share with God, Creation and one another is the inner journey we must make to the Central Altar of our temple. Along the way we allow the harmony of

Oneness and Love to form between our body, our Soul, and our consciousness. Qi Gong Practice is this journey into ourselves. The revelation of the Oneness and Love existing within our own being is the path to the oneness we share with God, all Creation, and each other.

As our consciousness moves toward Oneness and Love we begin to remember Who We Are. We come to understand what has occurred within us to cause our consciousness to contract. We recognize the ways our consciousness engages with the Qi of Creation and how these ways have caused us to experience realities in which we are separate from God, Creation, and each other; realities in which we are limited in our ability to love, and cut off from the infinite wisdom, power, and joy given to us by our Creator.

In discussing the Core Event, I have shared with you that Qi Gong Practice is Spiritual Practice. Its aim is our conscious union with God and Creation, and our conscious participation in our role as the sons and daughters of God. As I have mentioned before, understanding this does play an important role in the practice of Qi Gong. Understanding helps us to integrate our mind with our heart and body, and gives us both purpose and motivation in our practice.

Our Transformation ~ What is it?

Before I continue further into discussing the design of our temple and the keys of transformation and how we apply them, I need to bring forward a primary understanding that influences every aspect of Qi Gong Practice.

Our reawakening to Who We Are collectively and individually is the transformation of human consciousness. Now transformation is not the same as change. In change, we know what we are changing to; we are the doer, and we define and control our outcome. In transformation we do not know where we will end up. We invite the unknown to participate with us in our actions and allow this unknown to help and guide us toward the outcome. We are extending this invitation to the very power and intelligence creating and sustaining us moment to moment. This kind of action requires tremendous courage and, of course, trust.

We are presently living in a most sacred time. Our duality consciousness, an expression of consciousness based in a belief system of separation and limitation, is transforming into unity consciousness. This is the Consciousness of Christ about which I have been talking. This is the timing for the return of Christ Consciousness to earth.

We are going to a place that we are presently unable to conceptualize in our mind, and therefore it is not through our effort alone that this transformation takes place. Though it is realized within us, this transformation is a gift extended to us through the grace of higher vibrational consciousness. But, we cannot forget that we are beings of free will. We must ask for this transformation, and we must allow it.

In change, we know what we are changing to; we define and control our outcome. In transformation we do not know where we will end up.

Our acceptance of this gift, our gratitude, and our invitation to God and God Our Mother are the keys that open the door to our temple (ch. 12 "The Qi Gong State). How we walk the inner path to the Central Altar of our being is the practice of Qi Gong. The timeless wisdom of the practice guides our steps, reminding us Who We Are, and helping us to understand and apply the principles of love and the Keys for the Transformation of Human Consciousness.

Qi Gong Practice is not about our needing to do, learn, or accomplish more. It is not about acquiring more knowledge, skills, strength, or things. And the practice is not about our controlling or manipulating the Qi of Creation to bring about any of these things.

Qi Gong Practice is about our letting go, letting go of the attachments our consciousness has formed to a system of beliefs and experiences vibrating outside of the Consciousness of Oneness and Love. Our attachment to these beliefs and our attachment to the experiences of their realities, has kept us from experiencing a bigger truth. In the practice of Qi Gong, we consciously choose to release our attachment to the beliefs, attitudes and behaviors that need to control the Qi of Creation or need to get something from the Qi in order to be whole or gain personal worth. We let go of all the ways we hold ourselves ~ mentally, emotionally, energetically and physically, that block us from experiencing oneness, expressing love, and channeling the unlimited power of Creation.

We have been created to experience absolutely all of the infinite potential of God and its manifesting reflection as the infinite realities of Creation. But we have also been created to remember and experience the total truth of Who We Are. We are the Consciousness of God, and we are the Oneness and Love unifying God, Creation and Consciousness. Who We Are does not come from Creation, or from our experiences of Creation. Who We Are comes from God. Our love, wisdom, joy, power and health are inherent to our being. We are the limitless power to choose from the infinity of God and Creation the beliefs and stories we hold as our truth. Our truth then becomes our conscious experience of God, Creation, and one another.

Chapter Eight

Our Temple and the Sacred Altars Within

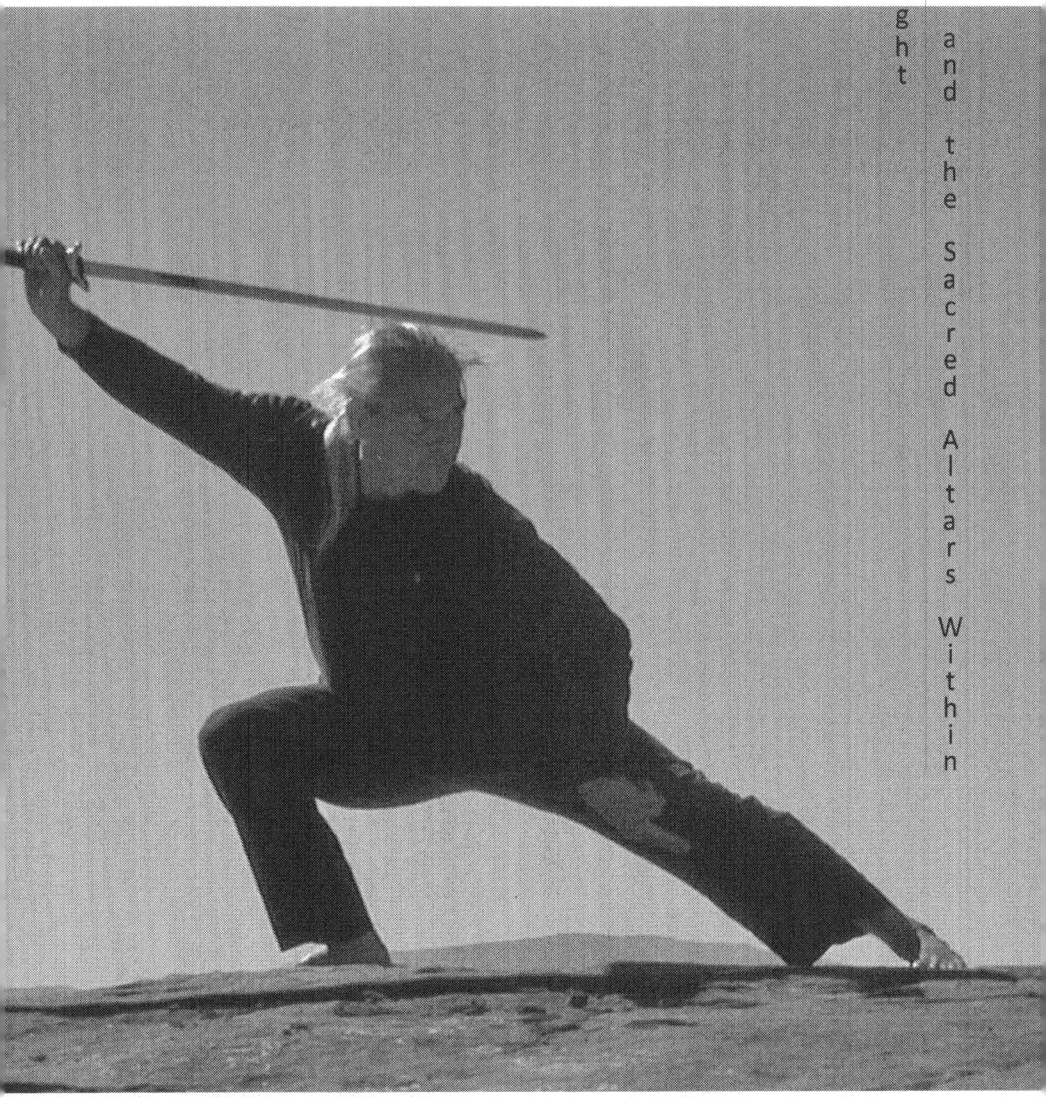

Creation Is God, Our Temple Is God, Our Soul and Consciousness Are God

GOD IS ONENESS AND GOD'S action is Love. God's act of Love ~ the sharing of oneself completely, springs forth naturally from God's Oneness. God's principle of Oneness is the template of love. It is the motivational power driving and guiding love's expression.

The trinity of God shows the ultimate Oneness of God choosing to share itself through love in three ways: the One Spirit of God, Creation, and Christ Consciousness.

In God's act of love, the act of creating, God shares all of its Oneness and Love with Creation and with the Consciousness of Christ. God's principle of oneness and expression of love therefore become Creation and the inherent quality of everything in Creation. And God's

Oneness and Love become Christ Consciousness and the inherent quality in all expressions of life. All that God creates also is the Oneness and Love of God; all that God creates is God.

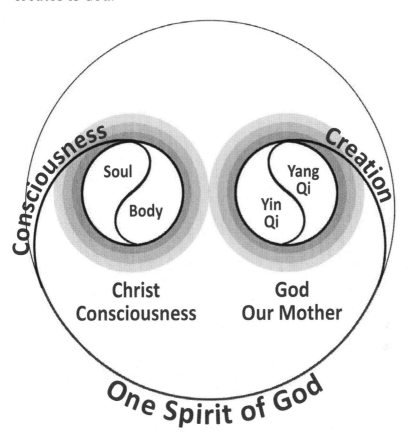

What is overtly clear in all of this is that the principle of oneness, and the expression of this principle through the act of love, is the key to God. Oneness and Love are the one underlying truth, and the eternal and seamless extension of God throughout all of God's Creation. For us, finding Oneness and Love is the truth that sets us free, giving us unlimited access to the totality of God.

In God's principle of Oneness, there is no separation, no less than, no lack of or need for, and no limited expression or limited possibility. The vibrational quality of Oneness and Love is all inclusiveness, equality, support of the infinite potential in all, and unrestricted giving and receiving of our whole and authentic self.

Being Oneness and Love, expressing Oneness and Love, and holding the vibrational quality of Oneness and Love as our truth, mark the way to the Central Altar of our temple. It is part of the sacred path by which we return to God. Our conscious experience of being this ultimate Oneness unifying all expressions of God is, as already stated, the Core Event of Qi Gong Practice.

The way to God, the conscious path of Oneness and Love, is not found outside of us. It is within us. Ours is an inward journey to rediscover the Oneness and Love that always exists within our being. This path leads us into the realms of our mind, our heart, and our energetic and physical bodies. Along the way, we are guided to consciously recognize what we have chosen to believe and invest ourselves in, and what we've held onto as our truth, on every level of our being. We are guided to see how we, based upon the beliefs we have chosen, are presently experiencing, interrelating, and interacting with God, with Creation, and with our sisters and brothers.

On this journey, we are invited again and again to sense the vibration of the one truth, the vibration of God's

Oneness and Love, emanating from our Soul and always reflected in all the levels of our being and in all the realms of Creation. In our experience of this vibration, we come to understand how our attachments to a belief system based in separation and limitation, and our attachments to our experiences of the realities that these beliefs have spawned, are obscuring and distorting our truth.

At a point along this path of revelation, we are given the keys to our transformation and guided in how to apply these keys within the sacred altars of our temple. These altars, formed from the three distinct vibrational fields of Qi, are the sacred portals by which our consciousness experiences, interacts, and interrelates with the Qi of Creation and the manifesting reflection of God within the Qi. It is through our application of these keys within our altars that we release our attachments to the beliefs and experiences that now no longer serve us.

Each one of us is a Christ Being and each Christ Being is the holy temple of God. What makes our temple holy is that it is the perfected embodiment of God, a perfected individualized vessel that not only carries the Consciousness of God into Creation, but also gives God, Creation and us the living experience of the Oneness and Love we all share.

We know that God has given all of itself to us; our Soul is God. We know that God has given all of itself to

Creation, for God Our Mother is God become manifest. Also being Oneness and Love, God Our Mother, too, has given all of herself in the creation of us. God Our Mother designed our being (Our temple) to be the perfect microcosm of her whole being, the macrocosm of all Creation. We must remember that God Our Mother is the Qi and the Divine Intelligence of Qi within which the reflection of God's infinite potential becomes the infinite realities of Creation. Our temple, therefore, being the absolute entirety of Creation, can also reflect the infinity of God. It is by way of this perfected reflection, formed in the individualized temple of our being, that the Consciousness of God is sustained inside of Creation as the Consciousness of Christ.

The design of our temple is such that we are made from every expression of God. "And God said, let us make man in our image, after our likeness...." (Genesis 1:26). Our Soul is the One Spirit of God, our body is the entirety of God Our Mother who is nothing less than God Become Manifest, and our consciousness, Christ Consciousness, is the Consciousness of God.

Our Being
and Its Sacred Altars

In the simplest of terms, our being is created in the balanced union of the One Spirit of God and Creation. This union is also seen as the marriage of heaven and earth.

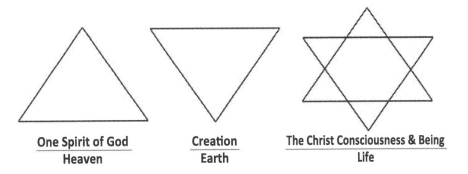

| One Spirit of God | Creation | The Christ Consciousness & Being |
| Heaven | Earth | Life |

Existing within the temple of our being are the three sacred altars, or tan tiens.

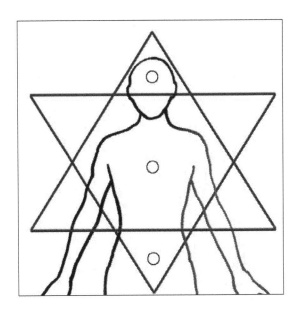

The three sacred altars of our temple are distinct, vibrational fields of Qi that facilitate all of the vital functions of our being. They are where the very purpose of our existence plays out. These three altars are not only the portals through which our consciousness experiences Creation; they also are the vibrational path that leads us to the conscious experience of our oneness with God and all Creation.

And then there is a fourth altar, the Central Altar of our being. This altar is the manifesting Oneness of God that arises within us out of the harmonization of our three sacred altars. This altar is our Spiritual Body and the access to our Soul. This altar is our oneness with God, Creation, one another, and all life forms.

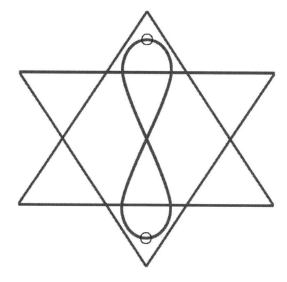

The Central Altar of our temple is the holy place in which the three expressions of God (The One Spirit of God, Creation, and the Consciousness of Christ) through love, consciously share their oneness. It is here that we experience the Core Event of Qi Gong

The Central Altar of our being is the manifesting oneness of God that arises within us. This altar is our Spiritual Body and the access to our Soul.

Practice. Within this holy place, we know that we are the Oneness and Love of God.

A little further along, I will return to this altar when we discuss how the Essence Movement of Qi Gong Practice frees the three sacred altars to harmonize with one another. Through this harmonization, the Oneness of God naturally arises within us.

The Relationship Between Our Sacred Altars and the Qi of Creation

As I return now to the three sacred altars of our temple, I will be touching back into the understanding of the three auras that form around the Flower of Creation and the Flower of Consciousness (ch. 2, pp 28-30).

The Oneness and Love of God and the infinite potential of God become manifest in the trinity of God Our Mother. She is Creation. Her body is the entire vibrational spectrum of Qi. Within this spectrum are three distinct vibrational ranges. These vibrational ranges of Qi form the three great realms or planes of existence ~ the Causal, Astral, and Etheric realms. It is throughout these three planes of Creation that the many kingdoms and many mansions of God are found. These realms are the layers of our Mother's body and produce the three auras surrounding the Flower of Creation. I find it helpful to picture these great realms as being like three octaves of music or better yet, a triple rainbow of light.

Our temple is designed by the Divine Intelligence of God Our Mother and, through her love, she gives all of herself in the creation of us. Her body becomes our body, and her great, vibrational realms of Qi become the three sacred altars within our temple.

The sacred altars of our temple are a microcosm of all Creation. They are three distinct vibrational fields of Qi that hold the template of our individualized being. Within these three fields the mental, emotional, and energetic layers of our body come into manifestation (it is within our energetic or etheric body that our physical body materializes). In this way, it is clear that the three altars within us are a manifestation of the oneness we share with the Causal, Astral, and Etheric realms of our Mother.

It is our mental, emotional, and physical bodies emanating outward from these three altars that form the three auras surrounding the Flower of Christ Consciousness.

Our Soul is God, our consciousness is the Consciousness of God, and our body, a gift to us from God Our Mother, is the reflection of God. Remember that the "gong" or the purpose of Qi is to reflect or bring into vibrational existence the infinite potential, the infinite beliefs and stories, of God. And remember that

I find it helpful to picture these great realms as being like three octaves of music or better yet, a triple rainbow of light.

our body, in all of its levels, is formed from Qi.

As the Consciousness of God, we are the ability to consciously experience and consciously interact with the manifesting image of God in the Qi of Creation. This is the very purpose of our existence. And we get to do this from the most unique perspective of our own, individualized temple. Our temple is a living vessel of Qi within Creation, giving our consciousness omnipresence, omniscience, and omnipotence throughout all Creation.

This is the unfathomable miracle of the three sacred altars of our temple:

- These three altars are the portals through which we receive our temple from God Our Mother.
- These three altars are the vibrational portals through which our consciousness opens to Creation. They open the way for our consciousness to experience the reflection of God within the Qi that forms our body, and that forms the great realms of Creation. Our three, sacred altars are what allow the infinite wonder of God to be our conscious experience.

Ultimately, the three sacred altars of our temple are the

vibrational manifestation of God's Oneness and Love within us. It is through the naturally-occurring harmony existing in and unifying these three altars that we come to the Central Altar of our being, access our Spiritual Body, and again know that God, Creation, and we, as the Consciousness of Christ, are one.

The Integration of the Three Altars
Within Each Level of Our Temple

The altars of our temple are absolutely magical. Each altar exists three times, being present within each of the three vibrational levels of our temple and performing a different function on each of these levels. In other words, each altar expresses itself within each of our three bodies, and each expression of that altar has a distinct function or set of functions. So you can see that we are actually talking about nine altars and at least nine different functions (most altars have more than one function).

Within each level of our temple or within each of our three bodies, the three altars (causal-mental, astral-emotional, and etheric-energetic) are always working in harmony with one another. Though each altar does have its individual role or function, the purpose and efficacy of that function comes through the harmonization of that function with the functions of the other altars. The realization of the greater work or mutual goal is always brought about through this integration of all three altars into a unified effort. This principle of the three altars combining into a single effort, of course, plays out within each of our three bodies.

In the practice of Qi Gong, this principle is often stated as, "What is happening on one level or in one tan tien is happening on all levels or in all tan tiens." A short example of this principle, showing the harmonization of the different functions of the three altars, would be my kicking a ball:

- In my Etheric-Energetic Tan Tien, which is also my physical center, I literally am moving my body to kick the ball.
- In my Astral-Emotional Tan Tien, which is my center of feeling, I am leading the energy within my body to kick the ball through how it feels to kick the ball.
- And in my Causal-Mental Tan Tien, my thinking center, I have decided to kick the ball, and in forming my intention to do so, visualize my doing it.

As the Christ Being and Consciousness, we exist in and experience all three levels of Creation. Our upper altar opens our consciousness to experience the Causal Realm, the realm of mental Qi (thought), and gives rise to our mental body. Our middle altar opens our consciousness to experience the Astral Realm, the realm of feeling Qi (feelings and emotions), and gives rise to our emotional body. And our lower altar opens our consciousness to experience the Etheric Realm, the realm of energetic Qi and matter (doing and being), and gives rise to our energetic and physical bodies.

Because each altar exists and functions within each level of our temple or within each of our three bodies, we experience influences of one level within the other levels. Within our causal-mental body, we have a mental, an emotional, and an energetic altar. Within our astral-emotional body, we have a mental, emotional and energetic altar. And within our etheric-energetic body, which is also our physical body, we also have a mental, emotional, and energetic altar. Each level of our existence therefore has a role to play in the other levels of our existence.

This integrative principle is an expression of God's Oneness manifesting within Creation and within us. It is also the result of the vibrational principle (or the natural laws) of harmonics. This is exemplified in music where a note or tone at one level in the scale activates or stimulates notes or tones at other levels (over tones). And then there is the underlying truth that all the tones and combinations of tones that can possibly exist are all expressions of the one vibrational energy of sound.

This naturally occurring principle of integration is a constant throughout all of Creation. It is present in the design of our being and is always at play in the way our consciousness experiences God in the vibrational realms of Qi. This principle of an underlying interconnectedness existing between all things of Creation is the basis of spirituality. All things are interconnected; everything comes out of the One Spirit of God. And finally, this principle of oneness is the constant in the practice of Qi Gong. It is the key through which we ultimately come

This principle of an underlying interconnectedness existing in the things of Creation is the basis of spirituality.

to know the oneness our consciousness shares with God and all Creation.

Another way we can see the integrative principle of oneness at play is in how the principles governing Qi itself hold true no matter the level or altar in which Qi is expressing.

A great example of this is the Qi's continual drive for balance. Within the triune or trinity expression of Qi, the yin Qi forces and yang Qi forces are always seeking balance in their giving and receiving of each other. If you will remember, the third force at play here is the Divine Intelligence of God Our Mother overseeing and coordinating this dance.

Within the etheric-energetic plane, the yang Qi expresses as a rising, expanding force and the yin Qi expresses as a sinking, contracting force. It is always in the balance of these two forces that the power for manifestation and all movement is generated.

Within the astral-emotional plane of our being, there is unimpeded movement of Qi and a natural releasing of stuck or stagnate feelings and emotions when we fully feel and accept all of our feelings and emotions. Feeling and accepting our feelings and emotions allows a natural balance to occur. This natural balance exists between the opposing or complementary forces of our feelings and emotions ~ between the complementary poles of desire and fear, happiness and sadness, acceptance and rejection, security and insecurity etc. But through our conscious and semiconscious repression of our feelings and emotions, and through our conscious and semi-conscious actions that erupt out of our over attachment to them, we have held our emotional forces in separation, trapping them in imbalance.

As we consciously choose to fully feel and accept our feelings and emotions, both their pain and their joy, we again bring the totality of our feelings and emotions into our consciousness. And it is here, within the light and presence of our consciousness that these emotional forces, trapped within their complementary or opposing poles, can truly reintegrate. This is an example of how the transformational keys in Qi Gong work when applied within this level of our being.

Within the causal-mental realm, clarity in our choices and decisions comes through an open and all-inclusive awareness of all thoughts arising around a particular subject or event, while then allowing a natural comparing to occur between these original thoughts and the complementary (or comparative) thoughts that also arise. In this middle ground, where these thoughts are allowed to integrate, new meanings, insights, and intentions are formed.

Another way Qi expresses balance and integration in the causal-mental level of our being is when we are simultaneously aware of our thoughts about the future and the past, while staying open to what naturally arises in the present.

AS I NOW DISCUSS THE FUNCTION of each sacred altar, I will be giving examples of how the principle of integration and oneness plays out upon each of the three levels of our being.

This part of the discussion does get a bit complicated. First I will give a brief overview of each vibrational realm of Creation and its corresponding altar within our temple. Then I will discuss the function of each altar in the context of how the role it plays within one of our bodies integrates with the functions of the other altars within that body. But because this principle of *the three altars integrating into a single effort* plays out within each of our bodies, I will actually be discussing the integration of the three sacred altars three times.

I once again ask you to remember that each of our sacred altars is a vibrational portal that opens the way for our consciousness to experience the reflection of God in the realm of Qi that corresponds to that altar.

The Causal Realm and the Causal Altar

The Causal or Mental Altar of our temple opens our consciousness to experience the Causal or Mental Realm of Creation. This realm, and therefore this level of our experience, is the infinite possibilities of God. Within the Causal Realm, the totality of everything we are, and the totality of everything Creation is and could ever be, is conceived or conceptualized in the mind of God. This level is comprised of the infinite beliefs and stories within God and our awareness of them as the infinite manifesting realities of Creation. In this level of Creation, we are aware of all possibilities.

The Causal is the realm of pure thought. Our experience of this realm includes choice, decision, and the formation of intention. The Causal Altar also gives our consciousness unlimited freedom to move through time. Metaphorically, the Causal Realm is the mind of God; it is where God touches our consciousness.

The Astral Realm and Astral Altar

The Astral or Feeling Altar of our temple opens our consciousness to experience the Astral or Emotional Realm of Creation. This realm and this level of our experience of Creation is about consciousness ~ **it is _all_ relationships.** The Qi of the Astral Realm is the interconnecting intelligence and energy creating and sustaining all relationships: the relationship between God and Creation and between God and us, the relationships between us and Creation and between one another, and all the different relationships existing between all of the life forms and things of Creation.

The Astral Realm is therefore how God, everything within Creation, and we, connect. And it is through our Astral Altar that we are aware of and participate in the infinite ways God, Creation, and we, as Christ Consciousness, connect, interact, share, and communicate with each other.

Our experience of the Astral Qi includes sensing, feeling, emotion, intuition, empathy, and compassion. The Astral Qi is the vibrational power of attention that carries or transmits our thoughts and intentions throughout our temple and all Creation. And the Astral Altar gives our consciousness unlimited freedom to travel in space and inter-dimensionally throughout all realms ~ throughout God's infinite heavens and mansions.

It is through the Astral that we share ourselves with God, Creation and one another ~ it is the medium of love. Metaphorically, the Astral Realm is the heart of God; it is from here that our consciousness reaches out to touch both God and God Our Mother.

The Etheric Realm and Etheric Altar

The Etheric or Energetic Altar of our temple opens our consciousness to experience the Etheric or Energetic

Realm of Creation. It is within the Etheric Qi that all things physical materialize. This realm, and thus our experience of this realm, is energy, matter, being, doing, and movement.

The Qi of the Etheric Realm generates the many expressions of energy that bring the great realms into existence, bring our temple with its altars into existence, and bring the infinite things in all levels of Creation into existence. These energies are what realize everything ~ they are what give form and function to the infinite possibilities of God. The Etheric Qi receives, is acted upon or affected by, the intentions and attention of God, us, and all life forms, bringing our joined will into manifestation.

The Etheric Qi gives rise to all of the expressions of energy that we experience including light, sound, electricity, magnetism, heat, movement and matter. It makes our sensory experiences of seeing, hearing, smelling, tasting and touch (pressure, texture, temperature, movement, position) possible.

It is through the Etheric Altar that our temple adapts to the reality or realities that we choose to occupy; it makes that reality real to us and makes us real in that reality. It places our consciousness into the continuum of Creation, allowing our consciousness to interrelate with all levels of Creation. Metaphorically, the Etheric Realm is the body of God; it is where God Our Mother cradles our consciousness.

Functions of the Three Altars Within the Causal-Mental Level of Our Temple

The Causal-Mental Altar of Our Causal-Mental Body

Here, I again remind you that in the creation of us, the Christ Being and Consciousness, God and Creation give all of themselves. We are all that God is and all that Creation is, and in our remembrance that Creation is God made manifest, we truly are the mind, heart, and body of God.

This first altar, or tan tien, of our Causal-Mental Body is our awareness of the infinite possibilities of God. Through this altar we are aware of the infinite beliefs and stories of God reflected in the Causal-Mental Qi as the infinite realities of Creation. In this altar, the choice of God to be the consciousness and living temple of Christ becomes us. And so it is here that we are aware of the possibility of our own existence and the possibility of the existence of all things ~ here we are aware of everything God is, we are, and Creation is.

But the Causal-Mental Altar is not only our awareness of the infinite possibilities of God; it also is the very possibility of choice. It is the possibility that we as consciousness can choose any of the infinite beliefs and stories of God and form the intention to consciously experience them as our reality.

So, the primary functions of the Causal-Mental Altar of

our Causal-Mental Body are to open our consciousness to the infinite possibilities of God and to give us awareness

In our remembrance that Creation is God made manifest, we truly are the mind, heart, and body of God.

of their manifesting reflections in the Qi of Creation. And then, through this altar, we exercise our most precious gift of choice, for we are the power that decides which realities we consciously experience as our reality. It is our Consciousness of Oneness and Love, shared with us by God and God Our Mother that guide us in this choosing.

The Astral-Emotional Altar of Our Causal-Mental Body

The second altar, or tan tien, of our Causal-Mental Body is the very possibility that we, as an individualized being and consciousness, experience relationship ~ that our consciousness can connect and interact with God and the infinite beliefs and stories of God reflected in the Qi of Creation. Through the Astral-Emotional Altar, we are aware of and experience all the possible forms of relationship, all the possible ways of interconnecting, interacting, sharing, and communicating that exist within God and Creation. This includes all the possible ways God connects, interacts, shares, and communicates with us and Creation, all the possible ways we connect, interact, share, and communicate with each other and Creation, and all the possible ways that all life forms and things connect, interact, share, and communicate with each other. Through this altar, we are aware of and experience all the possible ways consciousness inter-connects or joins God, Christ, and Creation.

This portal opens our consciousness to feel, intuit, and empathize with each and every life form and thing existing in all realities. This portal also is our power of attention that carries our thoughts, choices, and intentions throughout Creation. And it is the doorway through which our individualized being and consciousness travels to all the realms of Creation ~ to all of God's infinite heavens and mansions.

Finally, through the Astral-Emotional Altar of our Causal-Mental Body we sense God, sense our Soul, and sense God Our Mother (Creation). Our ability to sense the quality of God's Oneness and Love reminds us Who We Are. This sensing then informs our Causal-Mental Altar, and by so doing, helps and guides us in choosing the realities we consciously experience.

The Etheric-Energetic Altar
of Our Causal-Mental Body

The third altar, or tan tien, of our Causal-Mental Body is the very possibility that the reflection of God, as the infinite manifesting realities of Creation, can be real in our consciousness. It is the possibility that our awareness and experience of all the life forms and things (energies and matter) within these realities, and our experience of the infinite relationships within these realities, can be real... that our experience of the reality we choose can have a literal, tangible realness to us.

This altar is not about our awareness of the infinite real-ities, nor about how we choose the reality we consciously experience. This altar is about how our experience of the reality we choose can become real, literal, and tangible within our consciousness. This altar gives us the sense of sight, hearing, smell, taste, and touch on each level of our being. It is how our consciousness "touches" a reality, and how that reality "touches" our consciousness.

Through this altar, we can become real within any reality we choose, and that reality can become real within us.

It is the Etheric-Energetic Altar of our Causal-Mental Body that places us literally in the time-space continuum of Creation, giving us the possibility of being, doing, and moving within the realities of Creation. This altar gives our individualized being and consciousness the ability to adapt or vibrationally harmonize with any reality. Through this altar, we can become real within any reality we choose, and that reality can become real within us.

Let me use a voyage on a sailboat to the island of Kauai as an example of the three altars working together in the Causal-Mental Plane of our existence:

It is by way of the first altar, the Causal-Mental Altar, that our consciousness is aware of and experiences the possibility that we even exist, the possibility that there exists a reality in which there is an earth, a Pacific Ocean, wind, an island named Kauai, and that this reality contains sailboats, sails, and navigational knowledge and equipment.

This altar also is the very possibility that this reality, or any reality for that matter, can be chosen and that an intention can be set to consciously experience it. It is therefore through this altar that we choose to consciously experience the reality in which this voyage is possible.

In the second altar, the Astral-Emotional Altar, we are aware of and experience all the possible ways God and Creation connect, interact, share, and communicate with us and with all of the life forms and things within this reality. And through this altar we are aware of and experience all of the ways possible for us to connect, interact, share, and communicate with everything in this reality: our crew, the ocean, the wind, our sails and boat. The Astral-Emotional Altar also gives us awareness and experience of all of the possible ways the elements of this reality can interact with one another: how the temperature and pressure gradients produce the wind, how the water floats our boat, how the electromagnetic fields move our compass, how the algae produce the oxygen we breath, and how the plankton give life sustaining energy to the whales.

This altar is the very possibility that we, as consciousness, can become excited or impassioned about such a voyage. It is the possibility that our intention to make this voyage can be actually carried forward by the power of our attention (our will) to connect our consciousness to this particular reality where this information can then be delivered to the Etheric Qi.

And finally the third altar, the Etheric-Energetic Altar, is the possibility that any reality, and the things within any reality, including our own temple, do exist ~ not the possibility that these things can exist (Causal-Mental function), but that they actually, literally do exist. Upon receiving our intention to make this voyage, and also our excitement about doing it, the Etheric-Energetic Altar actualizes or makes the reality in which this voyage is possible real to us, and makes us real within this reality. Through this altar, we know the smell of the sea, the salty taste in the spray, the creaking of the hull in the rolling swells, and the brilliant, multicolored sunsets. The Etheric-Energetic Altar opens to our consciousness the possibility of being, doing, and moving within the time-space continuum of this chosen reality; it allows us to pull up the anchor, hoist the sails, and place our hand on the tiller.

Functions of the Three Altars Within
the Astral-Emotional Level of Our Temple

As we enter the Astral Plane of our existence, the function and focus of the three altars change from our awareness and experience of the infinite possibilities of God reflected in all Creation (the functions of our altars in the Causal-Mental Plane of our existence) to our awareness and experience of our relationships with God and God Our Mother (Qi) within the reality we have chosen to consciously experience.

A short overview of the functions of our altars in the Causal-Mental level of our being:

- *Causal-Mental Altar ~ our awareness of the infinite potential of God reflected in the Qi as the infinite realities of Creation. The very possibility that we, as consciousness, can choose a reality to consciously experience, and the possibility that we can then form an intention to follow through with it.*

- *Astral-Emotional Altar ~ the very possibility that our consciousness and being can experience relationship, and therefore, our awareness and experience of all the possible ways God, we, and all the life forms and things existing within the infinite realities of Creation connect, interact, share, and communicate with one another.*

- *Etheric-Energetic Altar ~ the very possibility that God's reflection as the infinite, manifesting realities of Creation, and all of the life forms and things abiding within these realities, do exist and can be experienced as real, actual, and tangible in our consciousness. And the very possibility that we, as an individualized being, can exist in these realities to be, to move, and do, therein.*

On the Astral-Emotional Plane of our existence, the three altars are vibrational portals by which our consciousness engages and interacts with the manifesting reflections of

God, the beliefs and stories of God that we have chosen as our conscious reality. And through these portals, our consciousness also interacts and participates with God Our Mother, the Divine Intelligence and power overseeing and coordinating the function of Qi within our chosen reality.

The three altars of our Astral-Emotional Body form all of the possible ways, within our chosen reality, by which our consciousness can connect, interact, share, and communicate with God, with God Our Mother, with our body, with one another, and with all of the life forms and things existing within this reality.

The Causal-Mental Altar
of Our Astral-Emotional Body

The first altar, or tan tien, of our Astral-Emotional Body links our existence within the Causal-Mental Plane of Creation to our existence in the Astral-Emotional Plane. This altar is the portal giving our consciousness mental function within the Astral Plane and mental function within the reality we have chosen to consciously experience.

Through this altar, we are aware of and experience everything that exists within the reality we have chosen. It is through this portal that we decide which things and life forms within our chosen reality we will consciously experience ~ what we will consciously activate and share our consciousness with; what we will actively engage and interact with.

In our present reality, we choose through this altar which parts of our reality, what life forms and things, we will experience, and decide how and to what extent we will connect, interact, share, and communicate with them. We choose if and how we will experience God and God Our Mother. And we select brothers and sisters with whom we will interact, share, and communicate, and how we will do it.

The mental function of the Causal-Mental Altar of our Astral-Emotional Body is the mental functions that we all recognize and are accustomed to. Within this altar, we compare one thought or group of thoughts to their complementary thoughts in a process of weighing and balancing. We accept and reject thoughts, and we combine these mosaics of thought to form meaning so that we can then make choices and decisions. And finally, through these mental functions, we set our intentions.

Here I feel it is important to clarify the differences between the mental functions occurring within the **Causal-Mental Altar of our Causal-Mental Body** *and the mental functions occurring within the* **Causal-Mental Altar of our Astral-Emotional Body.**

The functions of these two altars are similar, and yet they are different:

Functions of the Causal-Mental Altar
of Our Causal-Mental Body

- _Our awareness and experience of the infinite beliefs and stories of God, and their manifesting reflection in the Qi as the infinite realities of Creation._

- _Our ability to choose which of the infinite realities of Creation we will consciously experience as our reality._

Functions of the Causal-Mental Altar
of Our Astral-Emotional Body

- _Our awareness and experience of everything ~ all of the life forms and things that exist within the reality we have chosen to consciously experience._

- _Our conscious experience of connecting to or having a relationship with the reality we have chosen. In this quality of experience we move beyond just an awareness. We accept that the reality we have chosen is our reality and we choose to share our consciousness with this reality and its inhabitants._

- _Our ability to choose and decide which of all the life forms and things within our reality we will consciously experience, and how and to what extent we will connect, interact, share, and communicate with them._

When we focus in on the distinction between OUR

AWARENESS OF EVERYTHING THAT EXISTS [in the context of both the infinite realities of Creation, and all that exists within a reality]; and what it means TO CONSCIOUSLY EXPERIENCE THE REALITY WE HAVE CHOSEN, [to develop a conscious relationship with, to share our consciousness with, to consciously love, to consciously engage and interact with the life forms and things within our reality], we are really going deeper into understanding the different levels of our consciousness's experience, or the different ways that our consciousness experiences.

In this discussion, I have pointed out that our altars and their patterns of integration are our ability as Christ Consciousness to experience God and the reflection of God in the three vibrational realms of Qi. Our altars are the different levels of our consciousness's experience; they are the different ways that our consciousness experiences.

In the current understanding and vocabulary of psychology, these levels of our consciousness's experience are analogous to our Superconscious, Conscious, and Subconscious Mind. In comparing these two ways of categorizing the levels of our consciousness's experience, I include within the category of our conscious mind another level that I refer to as our *Semiconscious*:

Superconscious Mind
o The Mind of God

- The Causal-Mental, Astral-Emotional, and Etheric-Energetic Altars of our Causal-Mental Body.
  - Our awareness and experience of the infinite beliefs and stories of God as the infinite manifesting realities of Creation.
  - The very possibility that we as an individualized consciousness and being can exist.
  - The possibility that we can choose to consciously experience and that we can experience relationship with God, Creation, and one another.
  - The very possibility that the reflection of God can be real in our consciousness and we can be real in God's reflection.
- To some extent the Causal-Mental Altar of our Astral-Emotional Body
  - Our awareness and experience of all the beliefs and stories of God that manifest within the reality we have chosen to consciously experience.
  - Our memory of the previous times in which we have been awake, and therefore consciously living in the Oneness and Love we share with God and Creation.

Conscious Mind
- The Heart of God
- The Causal-Mental and Astral-Emotional Altars of our Astral-Emotional Body
- To some extent the Etheric-Energetic Altar of our Astral-Emotional Body
  - Our experience and interaction with the part of God and the part of our Soul that we believe we

are, and therefore, have chosen to consciously experience (what we are presently perceiving in the Qi of Creation and accept as our reality). This includes our thoughts, feelings and emotions, and our energetic/physical body. This also includes all of the life forms, energy, and matter we are presently aware of, perceiving them through our five senses.

Semiconscious Mind

~ *Our experiences of intuition and empathy with the life forms, energies, and things (matter) within our reality.*

~ *The memory of all that we have experienced in our past lives, and what we have experienced in this lifetime but have repressed due to the pain it has caused us.*

~ *Our connection to the collective consciousness of all human beings, and our connection to the consciousness of all life forms within our reality, including viruses & bacteria, all of the plant and animal kingdoms, and all of the kingdoms of life that we are only partially conscious of.*

Subconscious Mind

o The Body of God

o The Causal-Mental, Astral-Emotional, and Etheric-Energetic Altars of our Etheric-Energetic Body.

o To some extent the Etheric-Energetic Altar of our Astral-Emotional Body.

- Our connection to the intelligence, energy, and matter of the cells, tissues, and organs that make up our own energetic-physical temple.
- Our oneness with God Our Mother, Qi, and our oneness with the intelligence, energy, and matter of all Creation.
- How our experience of the reality we have chosen to consciously experience becomes real and tangible in our consciousness, and how we, as consciousness and a living being (temple), become real within this reality.

The Astral-Emotional Altar
of Our Astral-Emotional Body

I am now going to return to our discussion about the functions of our altars, specifically to the functions of the second altar, or tan tien, of our Astral-Emotional Body. This altar is the altar of altars because it is so dynamic with both extraordinary and ordinary functions.

Extraordinary Function

The extraordinary function of the Astral-Emotional Altar of our Astral-Emotional Body comes about through its close relationship to our Central Altar. Our Astral-Emotional Altar is like a harmonic echo or a vibrational sister to our Central Altar. If you will recall from our discussion about the Core Event (ch. 7), our Central Altar, though accessed through the harmonic blending of all of our altars on all of the levels they express, is another altar entirely. Our Central Altar is where the

Essence Movement takes us; it is where the Core Event happens, it is where we, as the Consciousness of Christ, consciously experience the Oneness and Love we share with God and Creation.

The extraordinary function of our Astral-Emotional Altar is its spiritual passage or opening to our Soul that allows our consciousness to sense our Soul and sense the Oneness and Love of God that we are. Through this opening, we sense the spiritual oneness connecting our consciousness and being to God, one another, and to all of the life forms and things (all the expressions of energy and matter) existing within our reality. Through this opening, we also sense the interconnecting oneness that exists between all of these things.

This spiritual opening that allows us to sense our Soul, and thus God, has some similarity to our ability to feel God through the Astral-Emotional Altar of our Causal Body. The big difference is that this extraordinary opening brings God and God's Love into our conscious mind, and into the reality we have chosen to consciously experience.

Because of this passage, we are reminded that we are God and we are love, all of the time. This gift of sensing the Oneness and Love that we are guides us and helps us in our everyday interactions, sharing, and communications with each other, and with the life forms and things surrounding us.

Ordinary Functions

The Astral-Emotional Altar of our Astral-Emotional Body has a grand variety of "ordinary" functions as well.

Relationship

Our Astral-Emotional Altar is the altar of consciousness, or the altar of relationship. Consciousness is the mystical, omnipresent medium or web connecting the One Spirit of God to us and all Creation. And consciousness is the medium interconnecting all of the life forms and things in Creation.

Our Astral-Emotional Altar is all of the relationships our consciousness has with everything that exists in our reality. Within it exists all of the possible ways our consciousness can share, engage, interact, and communicate with everything.

Our Astral-Emotional Altar is all of the relationships our consciousness has with everything that exists in our reality (or in any reality we choose as ours). Within this altar exists all of the possible ways our consciousness can share itself; all of the possible ways we can engage, interact, and communicate with everything within our reality.

Here we must remember that our ability to choose; the act of our choosing the life forms and things we consciously experience, and the act of our choosing the ways and the extent to which we share our consciousness with them, is a function of our Causal-Mental Altar. But it is our Astral-Emotional Altar that informs our Causal-Mental Altar as to all the ways our consciousness can relate to everything that exists within our reality, and about the principles that govern how we and everything in our reality share, interact, and intercommunicate.

So, the Astral-Emotional Altar within our Astral-Emotional Body is all the possible relationships and all the possible ways of interrelating within our reality. Moreover, our Astral-Emotional Altar is where and how we realize all of our conscious relationships. In this altar, we activate the ways we have chosen to share our consciousness and being; how we engage, interact, and communicate with the particular life forms and things we have chosen to experience.

Feeling

Where the Causal Realm is the realm of Mental Qi (thinking and thoughts) and the Etheric Realm is the realm of Energetic and Physical Qi (doing, moving, and action), the Astral Realm is the realm of Feeling Qi (feelings and emotions).

The Astral-Emotional Altar of our Astral-Emotional Body is our consciousness's ability to feel our reality. Through this portal we feel the vibrational information emanating out from the interplay between consciousness and Creation that takes place within the sphere of each life form. We also feel the divine information encoded in all expressions of energy and matter. This, of course, includes our ability to feel our own body and the living temples of our brothers and sisters.

Our intuitive feelings are God Our Mother's communications to us by way of our body. This is her direct route to us... We are therefore guided not only by God, but also by Creation herself.

Not so dissimilar to the extraordinary function of this altar that allows us to sense our Soul and thus God, its ordinary feeling function allows us to feel the Divine Intelligence and Power of God Our Mother throughout our reality.

We experience many kinds of feelings, but our feelings do fall into two camps: pure feelings and psychological feelings. In psychological feelings our consciousness is experiencing a blend of Mental Qi and Feeling Qi. In pure feelings, our consciousness's experience of feeling is not mixed with our consciousness's experiences of thought; the feelings are not arising from the functions of our Causal-Mental Altar (where we are choosing the beliefs and stories we hold as our truth).

We will talk about our psychological feelings in the next two sections; Heart Informing Mind and Emotions.

Our pure feelings can be further understood by seeing them as physical, physiological, and intuitive. Our physical and physiological feelings arise from our consciousness's interaction with our energetic-physical reality (Etheric Qi) and the inner workings of our energetic-physical body. Examples of physical feelings are our experiences of a place, an object, or another living being. Some examples of physiological feelings include our body's interactions with food and medications, or the ways a Qi Gong or Yoga posture can affect us. Hormonal and neurologic communications taking place within us are other sources of physiological feelings.

Our intuitive feelings are also pure feelings. These feelings are God Our Mother's (Creation's) communications to us by way of our body. This is her direct route to us. These feelings are usually guiding us along our life journey, informing us as to what is good for us and what is not.

What is good for us	What is not good for us
Harmony	Disharmony
Safety	Danger
Proceed	Stop or change direction
Pleasure/Comfort	Pain/Discomfort
Acceptance/Welcome	Rejection/Unwelcome
Desire	Fear
Attraction	Repulsion
Happiness	Sadness

This list goes on to include all the possible hues of complementary pairs of feeling.

Heart Informing Mind

Our psychological feelings arise from a blending of our Feeling Qi with the Mental Qi of our Causal-Mental Altar.

Here I will discuss the two primary ways we experience this blending.

In the first way, the blending or harmonization of Feeling Qi with Mental Qi permits our heart to inform our brain. It is a way by which our ability to feel the Divine Intelligence and Power of Creation (God Our Mother) helps facilitate the many functions taking place in our Causal-Mental Altar:

- Choosing the parts of our reality we will consciously activate… the life forms and things with which we will share, engage, and interact.
- Deciding how and to what extent we will share, interact and communicate with them.
- Choosing if and how we experience God and God Our Mother.
- Choosing which brothers and sisters we will share, interact, and communicate with, and deciding how and to what extent.
- All of the mental functions that we know so well:
  ~ The comparison of thoughts
  ~ The acceptance and rejection of thoughts
  ~ The formation of meaning (the combining of thoughts)
  ~ The setting of our intentions

This cooperation between the Astral-Emotional and Causal-Mental Altars, between Feeling Qi and Thinking Qi, helps us tremendously. It plays a part in how our Causal-Mental Altar chooses the beliefs (from the countless beliefs and stories manifesting in our reality) that we accept as our truth. We are therefore guided not only by God, but also by Creation herself in choosing what we activate and include in our conscious experience.

Emotions

Another way that we blend or harmonize Feeling Qi with Mental Qi is in the formation of emotions and feeling or experiencing our emotions through our Astral-Emotional Altar (our heart). Our emotions are formed in the bringing together of our thoughts and feelings.

Our Thoughts

- The beliefs and stories in God that we have chosen as our truth and that subsequently make up the reality we consciously experience.

Our Feelings

- Our extraordinary sensing of our Soul, and thus God.
- Feeling the vibrational information in all the life forms and the information encoded in all the expressions of energy and matter within our reality.
- Feeling our own temple (our body).
- Feeling Creation directly, feeling God Our Mother.

It is in this marriage of our thoughts and feelings, the formation of our emotions, that we, as the Consciousness of Christ, link to, form a relationship with, and even identify with the beliefs and stories we have chosen. Emotions are how our consciousness experiences and accepts these beliefs and stories as being our beliefs and stories. Through our emotions, the world we experience is felt to be our world.

The power in our emotions and the force that binds our thoughts to our feelings comes from us. It is the power

Emotions are how our consciousness experiences and accepts the beliefs and stories we have chosen as being our beliefs and stories. Through our emotions, the world we experience is felt to be our world... The degree of power our emotions have to affect, change, and control our consciousness is a direct result of the degree to which we choose to accept that our experiences of this reality create Who We Are.

given to us by God to choose. Our emotions arise from our consciousness's choice to believe that the stories we have chosen (and our experiences of these stories as our reality) have the power to directly affect, change and control our consciousness. In the formation of emotions, our consciousness even goes to the point of accepting that these beliefs and stories are our consciousness, that our experience of the reflections of these beliefs and stories in the Qi of Creation is where we come from and Who We Are.

Another way to say this is that our emotions arise from who we believe we are. And the strength of our emotions, the quantity or degree of power they have to affect, change, and control our consciousness is a direct result of the degree to which we choose to accept that our experiences of this reality create Who We Are.

Our emotions are like a two-edged sword. Separating the edges of the blade is an important line of balance and discernment. These two edges represent the extremes of the opposing beliefs that both become our emotions and inform our consciousness as to how to feel or experience our emotions.

Running along one side of this blade are the emotions we feel arising from the beliefs that we come from the reality we are experiencing, and that this reality is the power that affects, changes and controls Who We Are.

Running along the other side of the blade are the emotions we feel arising from the beliefs that we are God, the infinite source from which everything comes. And we are the Consciousness of God, the Christ Consciousness that has the power to choose the beliefs (from the infinite beliefs within God) we will consciously experience. But we must heed a caution here, for in the extreme of these beliefs it is possible to believe that we are not connected to Creation and our fellow beings. In this extreme we can feel that we are not touched or influenced by what we are experiencing. We can even go on to experience that we are not responsible for how our choices can and do affect Creation, others, and ourselves.

To perceive clearly the differences between these

foundational ways of believing that run along the two sides of this sword not only impacts how we feel our emotions, but is hugely significant in who we believe we are and our perceived purpose for being here.

We must heed a caution here, for in the extremes of this belief is also the possibility of our believing that we are not connected to Creation and our fellow beings.

The one system of belief leads us toward experiences of contraction and greater limitation, while the other leads us towards experiences of expansion and freedom.

If you will remember, we, as the Christ Being and Christ Consciousness are created in the union of God (our Soul) and Creation (our body). It is in their union that consciousness comes into being. The sacred key to sustaining the precious balance of Who We Are is our remembering that Creation (all realities) comes out of God; Creation is the reflection of God and the reflection of our Soul. God does not come from Creation, nor does our Soul come from Creation. Our consciousness is therefore God's Consciousness and what we experience in Creation (be it thoughts, feelings, emotions, energy or matter) comes from God and from our Soul. And it is we, as the Consciousness of Christ, who choose these experiences.

We have been created to experience all of the infinite wonders of God, to travel freely throughout God's infinite kingdoms and mansions, and share ourselves through love openly and completely with all Creation. We were not created to become entrapped, to have our consciousness yoked or attached to the Qi of any reality through a system of beliefs that would have us experience ourselves as separate from God, limited in our ability to manifest our will, and limited in our ability to share ourselves through love.

The line of balance and discernment running down the middle of the sword of our emotions marks a sacred path. This path shows us the way to fully and deeply experience the infinite realities of Creation while guiding and protecting us from becoming entrapped and limited within them. This path of balance and discernment is a part of the wisdom of Christ that has always been here and always openly shared with us and all life forms.

To enter the vibrational realms of Creation (the Causal, Astral, and Etheric Realms) is to feel emotions. It is important to understand that our emotions are not black and white; there are not good and bad emotions. As we walk the path of balance and discernment, we are guided to feel all of our emotions, to bring together and integrate the emotions arising from both sides of our sword. This is the wisdom of the path.

All of our emotions are a magical and awesome gift to us, enriching and deepening our experience of the manifesting reflection of God in the Qi of our reality. As we have already discussed, it is our emotions that connect us to the reality we have chosen. It is through them that we identify with our reality, feeling that it is our reality and that we are a part of it. Our emotions allow our consciousness to fully participate in our reality; they are the vehicle by which we engage and interact with the life forms and things coexisting with us.

Where as it is the Etheric-Energetic Altar that makes everything in our reality real to us and makes us real within our reality, it is our emotions, felt or experienced through the Astral-Emotional Altar, that truly bring our consciousness into this reality and make us feel that we are part of it.

The sword of our emotions is a divine tool giving profound depth and beauty to our experiences. But in feeling our emotions, we have over-attached and over-identified with both the Qi of our realty and our experiences of the beliefs and stories in the Qi. We have stepped too close to the edge of our sword and lost sight of the sacred path.

In our over-attachment and over-identification, we began to believe that our identity (Who We Are) and our value as a human being come from Creation and from our experiences of the beliefs and stories manifesting within her. We have even gone so far as to believe that we come from this reality, that it is our source. Through these beliefs, we now feel and experience that this reality and our experiences within this reality affect, change, and control Who We Are. We have literally entrapped and limited ourselves through our choice of beliefs and our subsequent experiences of their reflections in the Qi.

Our emotions are magic, all of them. Through our emotions we truly enter the reality that we choose to consciously experience. Our emotions are the sensitivity, intimacy, and passion in our experiences and make the experiences of empathy and compassion possible. Our emotions form a great part of our humanness. But through our emotions we can, and have, lost our balance and discernment. We have forgotten Who We Are.

Now is the time to bring our awareness into the feeling of our emotions. We must sense and feel the guidance coming to us through the wisdom of Christ, showing us how to again walk the path of balance and discernment.

The reflection of God and our Soul (which also is God) in the Qi of Creation does have the power to inspire our consciousness. The reflection of God and our Soul can persuade and dissuade our consciousness and the consciousness of others. But the Qi of Creation, and our experiences of the manifesting reflections of the infinite beliefs and stories of God in the Qi, have no power to change, control or harm the consciousness that we are. It is we and only we that have this power to change the state of our consciousness. And it is we alone that have the power to change both what we experience from God, and how we experience God's and our Soul's reflection in Creation.

Our emotions are the sensitivity, intimacy, and passion in our experiences and make the experiences of empathy and compassion possible. Our emotions form a great part of our humanness.

Another way this lesson shows up for us is in our relationships with our brothers and sisters, especially with those closest to us. We learn that we cannot change others just as others cannot change us. Again, it is only we who have this power to change ourselves. Yes, we can inspire others, and we can support them in their desire to change, just as we can be inspired and supported.

And so it is, through our own awakening, our own remembrance of Who We Are, that we most effectively serve each other, all life, all Creation, and God.

Attention

The last function of our Astral-Emotional Altar I will discuss is our attention or what we often refer to as our power of will. Our attention, or will power is the power of connection. It is the power connecting our Causal-Mental Altar (our mind) to our energetic and physical world.

Our attention carries the intentions of our mind into the etheric-energetic and physical level of our reality. In forming this connection, our attention delivers or transports this causal-mental information to its place of action and informs the Etheric Qi as to what action or work is desired.

Our attention also functions as a type of lens that can focus our awareness on to any specific part of our reality and, in doing so, intensify the delivery of our intention (our awareness and intentions are both Causal-Mental Qi). In response to this focusing and intensification of our awareness and intention through our attention, the Etheric-Energetic Qi aligns and concentrates into the specified area of our reality in order to bring about the desired manifestation or outcome.

The choosing of a specific place and a particular manifestation or outcome is, of course, the function of our Causal-Mental Altar. But the delivery of our intentions to our etheric-energetic and physical reality by our attention, and our ability to intensify the delivery of this Informational Qi by focusing, is the function of our Astral-Emotional Altar.

The Etheric-Energetic Altar
of Our Astral-Emotional Body

The third altar, or tan tien, of our Astral-Emotional Body is the portal through which our consciousness interrelates and experiences the Etheric-Energetic and Physical Qi of our reality. Through this altar we see, hear, smell, taste, and touch our own body. And by these same senses we experience the energetic and physical expressions of the life forms and things existing with us in our reality. The primary function of our Etheric-Energetic Altar is to make everything we choose to consciously experience real to us, and to make us real within the reality we have chosen.

Through this altar, God Our Mother as Creation gives us our three-layered temple of Qi, our own manifesting reflection. This holy gift of individualization makes possible the miracle of our existence. Individualization is the opening that brings our consciousness, in the form of a conscious living being, into the infinite beliefs and stories of God. Existing as the living Christ (as both being and consciousness within these beliefs and stories) we are given free reign to participate in all the realities of Creation. The Etheric-Energetic Altar gives our consciousness both place and time within the continuum of our reality, and through individualization we are given not only the expression of our being, but also the expressions of movement and doing.

God Our Mother is the Divine Qi from which all the intelligence, energy, and matter of Creation comes. And though God Our Mother as Creation comes out of God, as does our consciousness, Creation is not less than God. She is God become manifest. She is the feminine principle of God.

Creation's primary role, her gong, is to make manifest the infinite beliefs and stories of God (and of our Soul that also is God). But God Our Mother as Creation is also speaking to us; she is guiding and helping us. She is continually reminding us that we are love, we are one with God, and we are one with all Creation.

God Our Mother, like God, can speak directly to our consciousness. But she mainly speaks to us through the Qi that she is, the Qi that is forming our body and that is bringing all the life forms and things into being. This conversation is coming to us through our Etheric-Energetic Altar. Through this portal, our consciousness opens to the oneness we share with Creation for the temple (body) that she gives us contains the entirety of her being. This is her love in action ~ the giving of all of herself to us.

And lastly, our Lower Tan Tien, the Etheric-Energetic Altar within our lower abdomen, is known as "The Sea of Qi". It is here that the Qi of our being is stored. All of our movement and doing, and all expressions of our energetic and physical power originate and are coordinated by this altar.

The Etheric-Energetic Altar is our power to manifest. It is the focal point of the power and intelligence of Creation within us. Within this altar, Creation receives the beliefs we have chosen, the intentions of our mind delivered to her by the connecting power of our attention. And then, by bringing together, by harmonizing our intentions (Mental Qi) with our attention (Feeling Qi), the Divine Intelligence and Power of Creation within us (the Etheric Qi of our Etheric-Energetic Altar) gives energetic and physical form to our beliefs. And so it is that our beliefs become real to us in the Qi of our reality.

As it is for the Archer, so it is with us. For us to fulfill our purpose upon this earth, we must allow the altars of our temple to form their harmony of oneness.

A short example of how the three altars of our Astral-Emotional temple work together within our reality is the Archer. In order for the Archer to accomplish his task of hitting the mark with his arrow, the Qi of all three altars must unify into a single harmony.

In the Causal-Mental Altar or Upper Tan Tien, the Archer chooses his target from all of the possible targets. He finds its meaning for him and clearly sets his intention to hit the mark. He visualizes all the steps and the successful completion of his task.

It is through the Qi in the Middle Tan Tien that the Archer now aims his arrow. He focuses his awareness on the target, and thus intensifies his intention. Through his attention he feels the Qi of his being aligning, connecting him through the Qi of his bow and arrow to the target.

Informed by the Qi of intention carried within the Qi of attention, the intelligence and power of Creation within the Lower Tan Tien (Etheric Qi) receives and harmonizes the three expressions of Qi. Coming from his abdomen, power now fills the Archer's body to draw back the bow.

He releases, trusting the manifesting Qi to deliver the arrow to its destination.

Just as it is for the Archer, so it is with us. For us to fulfill our purpose upon this earth, we must allow the altars of our temple to work together. We must allow them to form their harmony of oneness.

The Three Altars of Our Etheric-Energetic Temple

The Etheric-Energetic Realm is the foundation of all Creation and the engine of manifestation. It is where the intelligence and power of God Our Mother (the intelligence and power that brings the beliefs and stories of God into vibrational expressions, into manifesting forms) reside. It is out of the Etheric Qi that all realms come into existence. Our temple too, with its many levels of Qi, comes into being out of this realm.

To us as the Christ Consciousness and Being, the functions of the three altars within our Etheric-Energetic (and physical) Temple are mainly semiconscious or subconscious. On this plane of our existence the intelligence and power of Creation is adapting our temple to the vibrational environments in which we choose to live. Each altar within our Etheric Body is an extension of God Our Mother through which she is coordinating our physical and energetic anatomy and physiology. She is constantly monitoring and adjusting thousands of life sustaining balances that support our living temple.

The Causal-Mental Altar
of Our Etheric-Energetic Body

The Causal-Mental Altar or Upper Tan Tien of our Etheric Body is centered in our brain. It reads and monitors the state of balance in the anatomical and physiological systems of our body. These include the integument, musculoskeletal, lymphatic, circulatory, respiratory, digestive, nervous, endocrine, and immune systems. This altar receives, through both neurons and hormones, information from every part of our body. This information is then deciphered, and a decision is made concerning what is needed to fine-tune the balances within these systems.

The Astral-Emotional Altar
of Our Etheric-Energetic Body

The Astral-Emotional Altar, or Middle Tan Tien, is the connection by which the intentions of the Causal-Mental Altar are carried into all parts of our energetic and physical body. This altar transmits the information concerning what must be done to the places within our temple where specific events must occur. These messages (intentions) are delivered through neurons and hormones to the skeletal muscles and the smooth muscles in the vessels and internal organs. This communication system also carries this information to the endocrine glands and directly to receptor sites on individual cells.

The Etheric-Energetic Altar
of Our Etheric-Energetic Body

The Etheric-Energetic Altar, or Lower Tan Tien, is the

energy and matter of our body. It provides the energy that brings about the literal movements (expansion and contraction, quickening and slowing) needed to sustain or restore balance in the functions of the bones, muscles, organs, vessels, glands, and cells of our body.

Upon receiving our mind's intention (delivered in the Qi of our nerves and hormones) the etheric-energetic intelligence releases the literal, tangible power of manifestation and action.

An example of the three altars working in harmony in our energetic and physical level of expression is the maintenance of healthy blood pressure.

The Upper Tan Tien receives either neurologic input from pressure receptors at different sites within the arteries or hormonal information from the organs regarding their adequate or inadequate profusion. The hormonal information originates primarily from the kidneys. The Mental Tan Tien deciphers this information and decides on a course of action (an intention).

The Middle Tan Tien then delivers this intention, carrying it to the heart, arteries and kidneys primarily through the nervous system, though some hormonal pathways are also used.
The Lower Tan Tien provides the energy and oversees the compensatory adjustments that take place in the heart and arteries and does the literal squeezing of endocrine

glands (adrenals) within the kidneys to release even more hormones that play into elevating and lowering blood pressure.

Blood pressure maintenance is but one example of the hundreds of life sustaining balances continually in adjustment within our human temple. Here are a few more:

Acid-Base

Insulin-Glycogen

$CO_2 - O_2$

Osteoclasts - Osteoblasts

Thyroid

Parathyroid

Immune System

Production & Reuptake of Neurotransmitters

Production & Destruction of Red Blood Cells

Stomach pH

Digestion-Elimination

The Power of Our Ego
Is Our Attachment to Untruths

GOD IS ONENESS AND LOVE. Creation is Oneness and Love. And it is Oneness and Love that God and Creation extend as our Soul, our body, and our consciousness. Our consciousness is the Christ Consciousness created in the holy union and shared love of God and Creation. Therefore, Oneness and Love is Who We Are in all aspects of our being, especially in our consciousness.

Knowing that we are Oneness and Love and being the living expression of Oneness and Love is the natural state of our consciousness. In this state (our awake or expanded state) we know and experience all life and all things through our Spiritual Body. Our Spiritual Body is the Central Altar of our temple where no separation exists between God, Creation, and our consciousness. Here we truly are God and we are all of God's Creation.

Knowing and being only Oneness and Love, as Christ, our true relationship to all things can only be Oneness and Love.

Our mind became the new god with dominion over the realms of our heart and body... We, as ego mind, do not trust our heart or body, we do not trust others, and we do not trust the very experience of life.

And yet, in our aspect of being the Consciousness of Christ, we have been given the gift of choice, the ability to choose any of the infinite beliefs and stories of God to be our conscious experience. If, in exercising this power, we choose to hold as our truth that we are something other than Oneness and Love, this also becomes our conscious experience. The danger here, as we are presently learning, is that in witnessing such an experience, we can forget Who We Are.

Right now we are choosing to believe that we are something other than Oneness and Love. We are choosing to hold as our truth that we are separate from God, Creation, each other, and all life forms. We are also choosing to believe that we are limited in our power to manifest our will, and limited in our power to love.

When we began to believe that we could be separate from God and Creation, separation and limitation became our experience. This belief began to inform our chosen reality; it became the nature of our reality. At the same time, we began experiencing ourselves as a separated being. This is when our Central Altar divided into

155

three altars, and we started to experience ourselves and Creation as existing on different levels - the levels of thought, feeling, energy and matter.

Now experiencing ourselves as existing in such a reality, our "I Am" consciousness, our Consciousness of Conscious Experience, identified itself primarily with the Causal Altar of our temple, the level of thought. As we identified more and more with the vibrational level of mind, we came to believe that our *true self* was our thoughts. Then believing that we were thought, we proceeded to judge our "thinking self" as superior to the other altars, therefore making our heart and body less important than our mind. Our mind became the home of our ego or separate existence; our mind became the new god with dominion over the realms of our heart (feelings) and body (energy and matter). This new god, our ego (or separate self) expressing as the thoughts dancing within our head, has become a fearful, judgemental, angry, and manipulative god. Having forgotten our oneness with all, and the interconnecting oneness within all things, our ego self now thinks, feels, and energetically and physically perceives that it is alone, cut off somehow from God, everything, and everyone. Forgetting that we are the literal source of all power, our ego also experiences that it is somehow cut off from the unlimited power flowing throughout our universe (Creation).

Feeling isolated, insecure, weak, and unsupported, our

mind falls into fear, the fear of its annihilation. Living in this survival mode we, as ego mind, cannot afford to trust anything. We do not trust our heart or body, we do not trust others, and we do not trust the very experience of life. No longer experiencing the integral part we play in Creation, we no longer trust the Divine Intelligence and Power of Qi (our Mother) to care for us and provide what we need and desire.

Motivated by this fear and distrust, we are obligated to push everything away, to experience it all as existing outside of us and separated from us. And, of course, the blame for our sad, sad condition must be outside of us as well with all of those other beings and things. We are then left with no other choice than to take the workings of Creation into our own hands and control the Qi. For in the fear-logic of our mind, if we were not controlling and manipulating Creation for our benefit, we would surely perish and have no meaning or importance.

The yin and yang forces of Qi are always seeking oneness through balance and integration. Our acts of control and manipulation serve only to interfere with this balance, distorting our experience of our true self. These distortions then go on to further influence us in our choosing of the beliefs we hold as our truth. In this contracted, myopic state of consciousness, we are not aware or sensitive to how our attempts to control Creation affect all of nature and all life. We also do not see that through these acts, we are attaching our identity and worth (who we believe we are in our consciousness) to the Qi and to our experiences of the reflections in the Qi. These reflections, remember, are only those beliefs and stories, from the infinite beliefs and stories within God that we have chosen to hold as our truth.

In spite of all of this… forgetting Who We Are, needing to control and manipulate the Qi of Creation, interfering in and distorting the balances and harmonies of nature, choosing to hold as our truth beliefs of darkness (beliefs and stories predicated on separation and limitation), and attaching our identity and worth to Qi and to our experiences of the reflections of these beliefs in the Qi… we are still Oneness and Love. We are God. We are God's Love. And we are God's unlimited power. This has not and cannot change. The only thing that has changed is who we have chosen to believe we are.

The Error Lies Only
Within Our Consciousness

Though our present experiences of being separate from God, Creation, and each other, and being limited in joy, wisdom, power, health, and the ability to love, come to us by way of the Qi, they are not caused by the Qi. If what we see or experience in the mirror of Creation is ugly, it makes no sense to blame the mirror. Creation and everything in Creation comes from God and our Soul. Creation is God become manifest. Qi is the divine medium that, in receiving God, brings the infinite unknowable and unexperiential into a knowable and experiential form.

She performs this miracle perfectly.

The reflections we experience in the Qi of Creation are not the cause of our experiences of being separate from God and limited in our power, as these reflections also come from God and our Soul (which is God within us). These reflections are simply manifestations of the beliefs and stories we have chosen from the infinite beliefs and stories of God.

No, the cause of our experiences of separation and limitation, of being something other than the Oneness and Love of God, lies in our consciousness. What we presently experience as our thoughts (the reflections in the Causal Qi), feelings (the reflections in the Astral Qi), and perceptions of energy and matter (the reflections in the Etheric Qi) are the effects of both who we choose to believe we are in our consciousness (which is how we choose which of the infinite beliefs and stories of God we will consciously experience) and the kind of relationship we, as consciousness, choose to form with the Qi and these reflections.

To clarify, let me state this in another way. All of our experiences, no matter on which vibrational level they occur (mental, feeling or energetic) are simply effects. The cause of these effects is our consciousness, for our consciousness is the ultimate power of choice over what we experience, and over how, as consciousness, we define our relationship to these experiences.

Who We Believe We Are

How we, as con-
sciousness, choose to
relate to our experi-
ences feeds back into
our consciousness to
influence our beliefs
about Who We Are.

It is both the reflec-
tions of the beliefs
we choose and how
we choose to relate
to the Qi and to these
reflections in the Qi,
that form our experi-
ences.

Who we believe we are
guides us in choosing
the beliefs and stories
that are then reflected
to us by the Qi as our
thoughts, feelings, and
perceptions of energy
and matter.

Who we believe we are
also defines how we, as
consciousness, relate to
the Qi and to these
reflections in the Qi
of thought, feeling,
emotion, energy, and
matter.

The beliefs we hold in our consciousness about Who We Are guide us in choosing, from the infinite beliefs and stories of God, those beliefs that become the reflections we consciously experience in

If what we see or experience in the mirror of Creation is ugly, it makes no sense to blame the mirror... The cause of our experiences of separation and limitation lies in our consciousness.

Creation. These reflections are our thoughts, feelings, emotions, and perceptions of energy and matter. Who we believe we are guides us in the kind of relationship we choose to form with the Qi and with these reflections of thought, feeling, emotion, energy and matter.

It is actually both of our choices: our choice of beliefs that become the reflections in our thoughts, feelings, emotions, and perceptions of energy and matter; and how we choose to relate to the Qi and to the reflections of these beliefs in the different vibrational levels of Qi, that form our experiences. And it doesn't stop there, because ultimately it is how our consciousness chooses to relate to our experiences that feeds back into our beliefs about Who We Are. That is how the circle of belief, choice, and experience loops back to belief, and keeps on rolling.

It all really does come back to this. The root cause of every one of our experiences is who we believe we are. Our beliefs about Who We Are choose what we experience. They define our relationships to God, Creation, and our brothers and sisters, and subsequently form our experiences of them.

~ What beliefs are we choosing to hold on to now?

~ Who do we believe we are?

~ What have we substituted for the eternal and unlimited love unifying God, Creation, and the Consciousness of Christ?

What we now believe, and therefore what we are presently experiencing, is that our identity (Who We Are) and our value as a human being come from the Qi and from our experiences of the reflections in the Qi. This choice to attach our identity and value to the Qi and our experiences of these reflections has yoked our consciousness to a reality that reflects these beliefs. This attachment has caused our consciousness to contract, keeping us in this contracted state for a long, long time. This is the "Catch 22" or the feedback loop we have trapped ourselves in. We experience what we choose to hold in our consciousness as our truth (who we believe we are) and then attach our identity and value to the manifesting reflections of these "truths".

As we recognize what is happening in our life, accepting that we are responsible for our experiences, and that what we are choosing to believe in is our experience of life, we deepen into ourselves. We more deeply ask, "What do I believe in?" Then, more precisely seeing what these beliefs and experiences are that we are choosing and giving ourselves to, we must go even further and ask, "How is it or how does it happen that I continue to hold on to and invest myself in these beliefs?"

The answers to these questions have, up to this point, been the primary thrust of this treatise. It is all about our consciousness and the God given power of our consciousness to choose, from the infinity of God, how we define ourselves. We choose the beliefs about Who We Are, and who we believe we are sets the vibrational quality or level of our consciousness. This vibrational quality of our consciousness now is the precedent for each of our subsequent choices of belief and colors every one of our experiences. Who we believe we are is the quality we infuse into our every experience; who we believe we are is the vibration with which we construct our entire belief system.

At this point, we are more clearly seeing what we have chosen:

- We have chosen to believe that we are separate from God and Creation and our fellow beings.
- We are limited in our power to love and manifest our will.
- We have chosen to believe that our identity and value come from the Qi and from our experiences of the reflections in the Qi.

But to the question regarding how is it that we continue to invest ourselves in and perpetuate these beliefs, there is another subtle aspect. Judgement.

Judgement

As we experience the reflections in Creation of the beliefs we have chosen, we are not simply experiencing.

We are seeing these reflections through eyes of judgement. Of course, this judgement is not in our eyes or in our ears, nose, mouth or sensory nerves for that matter. This judgement is in our belief about Who We Are, and it is in the vibrational quality of our consciousness. This act of judgement that we have formed has become a lens covering the three altars of our temple, distorting our every perception of God, Creation, and our fellow beings. Our action of judging is another way that we continue to link or bind our consciousness to the beliefs we have chosen, to the Qi, and to our experiences, for what we are judging is our experiences of the reflections of these beliefs in the Qi.

In judging, we are projecting our consciousness into the Qi through our need to hold on to and control the Qi and the manifesting images within her (according to what we believe is right and wrong). Through this act, we literally divide each of our experiences and invest our consciousness into this division. We seek to give our Spirit or life force to what we believe is right, and withdraw our Spirit from what we believe is wrong. This is how we presently believe we will reach God and slay evil.

Our beliefs about right and wrong, good and bad, beautiful and ugly can only exist in a reality reflecting the limited beliefs that we are separate from God and Creation. Our actions of judgement are based in how we believe the things and beings around us either benefit and augment us, or hurt and diminish us, neither of which is based in truth. Our choice to judge only continues our attachment to this false system of beliefs.

The beliefs and stories we are now choosing to hold as our truth, and the resulting experiences we are attaching

We are not simply experiencing. We are seeing these reflections through the eyes of judgement. This judgement is in our belief about Who We Are; it is in the vibrational quality of our consciousness.

to, are not our core truth. Our identity and value come directly from God. Our value cannot be separate from our identity that is the Oneness and Love of God, the Oneness and Love that unifies our Soul (the One Spirit of God), body (all Creation) and consciousness (the Consciousness of Christ).

Our release of the attachments we have formed to the Qi and to these experiences is the Essence Movement of Qi Gong Practice. I will soon be discussing this deep movement that takes place within the three sacred altars of our temple. It is what carries us back to the Central Altar of our being where the Core Event of Qi Gong Practice takes place. The point I do want to make here is that the cause of the Essence Movement is our remembering, our conscious knowing again that we are Oneness and Love. In our conscious choice to realize this truth, we naturally choose to divest ourselves or release our consciousness from that which is not our truth. We naturally make untrue all experiences that are not informed by the God intelligence of Oneness and Love.

Reawakening Is a Gift
Given to Us by God, Through Creation,
with the Assistance of Christ

Also being of God, the Divine Intelligence of Creation is always leading us back to Oneness and Love. And so it is that even the fear and pain we experience while under the spell of our ego, the untrue belief of a separate and limited self we have chosen to hold as our truth, move us toward our core truth.

Each of us comes to the pivotal point in our life where the fear for our survival and the pain of an existence without importance and meaning impels us to ask those essential questions (or a version of them):

Who am I?

What is my role in this life?

How am I to live this role?

But where or to whom do we turn when we decide to seek out the truth about Who We Are and what our role is? The help and guidance we need can only come from outside of the self-perpetuating belief system we have chosen, and from outside of its reflection (the reality in which we have entrapped ourselves). It is to our Soul, to the Oneness and Love of God within us, that we must turn.

- Our Soul is Our God Self.
- The Qi of Creation is always leading us to our Soul.
- The journey of our reawakening is a journey to our Soul.

- The application of The Keys For The Transformation Of Human Consciousness (The Essence Movement of Qi Gong Practice) is our letting go of everything that stands between us and our Soul.
- Our remembrance is our conscious experience of being our Soul.
- Christ Consciousness is our conscious experience of the purest reflection of our Soul in the Qi of our Spiritual Body (the Core Event of Qi Gong Practice). In this experience, we again consciously know we are the Consciousness of Oneness and Love unifying our Soul (God), our body (Creation), and our consciousness (Christ Consciousness).

The conscious act of asking for help and guidance in our life always elicits a response from our Soul. This response always reveals to us the absolute truth of Who We Are ~ we are Christ. In truth, the answers to the three essential questions are quite straightforward:

1. Who are we? We are God; we are Oneness and Love.
2. What is our role? Our role is to remember that we are God and to be the living expression of Oneness and Love upon this earth.
3. How are we to live this role? By taking the path that our Soul extends to us by way of God Our Mother, the Divine Intelligence and Qi of Creation. This is the path, if we choose to walk it, that leads us out of our experiences of being separate from God and limited in our power to love.

As I shared earlier, these three questions serve as guideposts on the path of Qi Gong Practice. They not only guide us to the doorway of our temple, they also mark the inner journey to our true self. On this journey, we ask our Soul for help and guidance. We must allow and trust the Divine Intelligence of God Our Mother (the Qi of Creation) to bring us our Soul's response. We also can accept the help of Christ, the living wisdom of our brothers and sisters who have come here to show us the way. And we must have the courage to receive this help and guidance ~ the courage to live in a new way, the courage to take an unknown path laid before us by God, God Our Mother, and Christ.

Yes, our Soul always answers us, and this response will always reveal the truth of Who We Are. How this truth comes to us, and how this truth translates into the experiences of our everyday life is Qi Gong Practice.

Remember that our enlightenment or reawakening is a gift given to us by our Creator (by our Soul, the Oneness and Love of God within us) through the Grace of God Our Mother, with the help and guidance of our Christ Brethren. An important part of this gift comes to us by way of the inherent design of our mind. The nature of our mind is that it can choose any of the infinite beliefs and stories of God to be our conscious experience. This function of our mind has no limitation. And yet, at the same time, the nature of our mind is that it cannot serve two masters. Our mind will not serve both truth and untruth. And therefore, as the core truth of Who We Are is revealed to our consciousness, the untruth of separation and limitation ceases to exist as our conscious experience.

We must allow and trust the Qi of Creation to bring us our Soul's response. We must have the courage to live in a new way, the courage to take an unknown path laid before us by God, God Our Mother, and Christ.

In our remembering that we are Oneness and Love, we release our attachments to the Qi and to our experiences of the reflections of separation and limitation in the Qi. We again start to choose beliefs and stories that harmonize with our core truth. We consciously choose to experience the oneness we share with God, with our Divine Mother, and with our Christ brothers and sisters. And we choose to express love, the Love of God that gives all of itself to all that it creates.

Being Christ Consciousness, we have been created to consciously experience all of God and Creation. Our ability to consciously experience God and Creation through the altars of our temple is quite literally God and Creation's conscious experience of one another. As we share our experiences with them, we form the link that completes the circle of their conscious loving of each other.

So, at some point in this journey of self-revelation and realization, we come to see that we are the holy gift we give back to God and Creation. We come to see that we are the holy gift we give to our brothers and sisters.

Experiencing Gods Reflection | The Power of Our Reality Is Our Belief in It

And finally, through this sharing of ourselves with God, Creation, and our bothers and sisters, each one of us realizes that we are this love, and worthy of receiving this most holy gift from ourselves.

SIMPLY PUT, QI GONG PRACTICE is the way of Oneness and Love. It is the natural way that we, as Christ, express within creation; it is the way we consciously live our oneness with one another, and with all the life forms and things in our "world". But when we have forgotten Who We Are, when we have lost our way in dreams of being separate from God and limited in our power to love, Qi Gong Practice then becomes the way back to our God Self. It becomes the spiritual language that communicates Oneness and Love to us, and the inner path by which we can return to Oneness and Love.

It is our Soul that extends to us the practice of Qi Gong, but the practice itself is formed within the Qi of Creation. Yes, Qi Gong Practice exists within the Qi. But, remember that God Our Mother is the Qi of Creation. Her intelligence and power are the vibrational manifestations of God. God Our Mother also is the Holy

Spirit spoken of in Christian and Jewish doctrine.

The beauty and genius of Qi Gong Practice as a spiritual language and path is how it reaches our consciousness through every vibrational level of our existence. Qi Gong is simultaneously occurring in every altar of our being and always leading us to the Central Altar, our Spiritual Body. It is the language of Qi Gong Practice that brings us the Keys for the Transformation of Our Consciousness, and it is the path of Qi Gong Practice that we walk as we apply these keys to the circumstances of our present life.

When we have forgotten Who We Are, Qi Gong Practice becomes the spiritual language that communicates Oneness and Love to us, and the inner path by which we can return to Oneness and Love... The beauty and genious of Qi Gong Practice is how it reaches our consciousness through every vibrational level of our existence.

When we ask the essential questions (Who am I? What is my role in this life? How do I live this role?), we are asking from the level of our Consciousness of Conscious Experience. This state of consciousness is our separate, ego consciousness or "I Am" consciousness. In this consciousness (also called Duality Consciousness), we experience ourselves as being unique, and as having an individually, unique experience and perspective of God and Creation. It is also in this duality consciousness that it has been possible for us to experience ourselves as being separate from God, one another, and all the life forms and things within our reality.

It is therefore here, within our present state of consciousness, that we must first receive the answers to the questions we have asked of our Soul. We receive these answers primarily through the Qi of Creation in the form of our thoughts, feelings, and perceptions of energy and matter. We also can and do directly sense our oneness with our Soul and God Our Mother through the extraordinary function of our heart and through our body.

Qi Gong Practice is the language and the path that bridges this apparent abyss between our Conscious Experience of Being Consciousness (which is our natural state of oneness with God, Creation and our sisters and brothers) and our Consciousness Of Conscious Experience, which is our present dualistic state of consciousness in which we experience ourselves and all things as being separate and limited, and uniquely so.

So, as each one of us comes to the pivotal point in our life where we consciously decide to know Who We Are, we literally root or ground one end of this bridge into our life. We consciously accept God and the Divine Intelligence of Creation into our life; we enter into a conscious conversation with them and with our Christ brothers and sisters who have walked this path before us.

Each of us has chosen to attach our consciousness to something other than Oneness and Love, and each of us has done this in our own way. Our present reality is formed from the beliefs and stories we have all chosen to hold, our collective beliefs, but each one of us has also brought into this reality beliefs and stories that we have uniquely chosen to hold as our truth. What this means for us as we walk the path of Qi Gong Practice is that even though God, Creation, and Christ give to us their divine knowledge and wisdom, we really can only receive this help and guidance within the context of our present reality, and more specifically from within our particular version of it. We must begin, and can only begin our reawakening from the unique place we occupy now.

It is for this reason that Qi Gong Practice reveals to us our truth in both the broad sense of Who We Are as a human being, and also in the specific sense of the individually unique path that our Soul holds for us. In other words, the information we receive from our Soul and Christ by way of the Divine Intelligence of God Our Mother comes to us in two parts:

- We are given the highest metaphysical truth, which is God's perfect and only belief about Who We Are. This is the theoretical knowledge of Qi Gong Practice.
- We are given the mundane truth (also coming from our Soul or God) that holds the specific reasons we incarnated. It is our Soul's memory of what we have come here to do and how to do it. This is the wisdom and the method of Qi Gong Practice.

Our mundane truth is the *what-when-where-how-with whom* information of our individual life. It is our strengths and weaknesses, gifts and wounds. And it is the specific help and guidance that we receive from our Soul, God Our Mother, and Christ as it applies to the unique ways each of us has attached our consciousness to this reality. This wisdom brings to us the Keys for the Transformation of Our Consciousness and shows each of us how to apply these keys to the unique circumstance and situations of our daily life.

The primary intention of Qi Gong Practice is to help us remember that we are Christ. In this conversation we are continually reminded that we are God, we are God's Consciousness, we are God's Creation, and we are the Oneness and Love of God unifying it all.

The primary method of Qi Gong Practice is its Essence Movement: our conscious application of The Keys For The Transformation of Human Consciousness within the altars of our temple. It is here, within the sacred altars of our being that we, if we so choose, are shown how to release our attachments to every belief, thought, feeling, emotion, and expression of energy and matter that stands between us and the Oneness and Love of God that we are. The practice of Qi Gong is always teaching us how to consciously experience the reflection of any aspect of God we choose, while reminding us that we do not come from the Qi, nor from any of our experiences of these reflections. We are the infinite source from which the Qi and all of these reflections come, and the eternal witness to it all.

In summary, Qi Gong Practice is spiritual practice. It is a gift given to us by God through Creation. When we chose to attach our identity and value

The practice of Qi Gong is always teaching us how to consciously experience the reflection of any aspect of God we choose, while reminding us that we do not come from the Qi, nor from any of our experiences of these reflections.

to beliefs and stories vibrating outside of God's truth of Oneness and Love, our state of consciousness fell. At this juncture, Qi Gong Practice has become the gift of remembrance, the gift of our return to Oneness and Love.

This remembrance is forever held for us in God and in the Consciousness of Christ, and is extended to us as we ask for it through the Grace of God Our Mother. Qi Gong Practice is the language by which this gift is given, and the path leading us back to our conscious experience of being-at-one (atoning) with God.

As we walk this path, the path of a spiritual life, we come to see that God is extending itself into us eternally. Never were we separate from God nor could we ever be. Therefore, in our journey back to Oneness and Love, we are guided and shown how to untie our consciousness from untrue beliefs and their false realities. We are shown how to release our attachments to the many versions of the belief that we have to do something to, control something in, or get something from Creation in order to define Who We Are and earn or gain our value.

Though this belief and versions of it appear to exist, they do not. They can appear to exist and can appear to be real to us only to the extent that we choose to share ourselves with them. It is our choosing them, and our choosing to hold on to them as our truth, that gives them "realness".

On the path of Qi Gong Practice, we are reawakening to the truth of Oneness and Love, and remembering that this is Who We Are. In the Essence Movement of the practice, we are quite simply letting go and surrendering. We are choosing to let go of that which is not based in our truth, our deepest sense of Oneness and Love, and we are surrendering to what remains. What remains is the very source of Who We Are, the One Source from which everyone and everything comes.

180

THE THIRD PART
of the
THREE PART STORY

How I Remember

WITHIN EACH OF US

OUR DESIRE TO KNOW AND our will to seek out Who We Are bring us to the practice of Qi Gong. This desire and will bring us to the doorway of our temple. But it is by entering into the Qi Gong State that we open the door.

The Qi Gong State is the opening prayer through which we enter each session of Qi Gong Practice. The intention of this prayer quite literally sets the vibration that reveals to us the internal path, places us upon this path, and opens us to receive the help and guidance coming from our Soul and from Christ through the medium of Creation. We but need to "Ask, and it shall be given you...; Knock; and it shall be opened unto you." (Mathew 7:7)

The ingredients of this prayer are Acceptance, Gratitude, and Invitation. I include here the prayer I use to enter into my practice sessions, but any prayer containing these ingredients will work:

Infinite God, Creator of All, the One Spirit

Divine Goddess, God become manifest,
the Divine Qi from which all of the intelligence,
energy, and matter of Creation arises.

And Christ, the holy consciousness and being,
created in the union of God our Father
and Creation our Mother:

~ Who we all are
~ Who the great ones are
~ And who I, too, am.

I love you and thank you for all that I am,
all that surrounds me,
and all that you have revealed to me.

I ask for your help and guidance in my life
and in the lives of all beings.

Acceptance

In this act, we are choosing to accept many things on many levels. But we must start by recognizing to the best of our ability what is happening in our life now, and accept that this is what we have chosen to consciously experience as our present reality. This means that we do not deny what we are experiencing no matter which level it is happening on (mental, feeling, energetic, or physical), nor do we deny its effects on us. And we do not suppress or hide these effects within us. This is the acceptance of what is now. This acceptance empowers us to take back responsibility for our experiences and opens a way for us to choose again with the guidance and help of God, Creation, and Christ.

Our access to God, Creation, and Christ is only through the present moment. As consciousness, we cannot commune with them in the future or the past, for in God these separations of time do not exist. We, therefore, practice Qi Gong in the present moment. When we do not accept what is now, whatever that may be in our present life experience, we have no starting point, and cannot place our feet upon the inner path, do Qi Gong Practice, or find the access to our true self. Without this acceptance we just stay trapped. We continue in our attachments to the many illusions of "what if":

• What if I had done this or not done that
• If only this or that had been different
• What if I were to do this or were not to do that
• If only this or that would be different

These attachments, again, only serve to keep us from the present moment.

In this level of our accepting, we accept everything we experience, including our experiences of separation, limitation, inadequacy, failure, sadness, and pain, as well as our experiences of oneness, love, wisdom, power, success, abundance, joy, and pleasure. Here we also recognize and accept our strengths, talents, and skills as well as our weaknesses, faults, and disabilities.

Creation's intention (a part of her gong or purpose) is always to guide us back to our truth... Every experience is part of God and Creation's message of salvation.

The central piece in our acceptance is to accept Who We Are and all that is being revealed to us by the Divine regarding Who We Are. We accept that in our creation, God and Creation gave and continue to give all of themselves to us. We therefore are all of God and all of Creation, eternally.

We also accept that in the creation of Creation, God extended and continues to extend all of itself to her. Therefore, Creation, too, is all of God's Oneness and Love. In this acceptance we know that Creation's intention (a part of her gong or purpose) is always to guide us back to our truth.

And finally, we accept that our reawakening into God is a gift, given to us by God, through the grace of Creation (God Our Mother or the Holy Spirit), with the assistance of Christ.

Gratitude

Our thanks is for everything ~ all that we are, all that surrounds us, and all that is revealed to us.

We give thanks for the gift of our reawakening, the eternal memory of Who We Are, held in our Soul and communicated to us through the Qi of Creation. And we give thanks to Christ, for the wisdom our Christ Brothers and Sisters share with us along our journey.

Our gratitude is also for every experience, every perception and interaction we have, for absolutely everything we experience is our path. Every experience is part of God and Creation's message of salvation. Every experience holds the opportunity for us to remember Who We Are.

Invitation

We invite God, Creation, and Christ to participate in our life. We ask them to help us and guide us that we may know again that we are the Oneness and Love of God, the living expression of God's Love on this earth.

We Are the Precious Balance
Formed from God and Creation

WE HAVE DISCUSSED AT LENGTH Who We Are. The memory of Who We Are, both as a human being and as a unique expression of God with an individually unique path, is the metaphysical knowledge shared with us in the theory of Qi Gong. How we remember, and how we actualize this memory, as a living God Being, is the method of Qi Gong Practice.

The method of Qi Gong Practice is the focus of these last six chapters, starting with The Qi Gong State. As we just discussed, the Qi Gong State is how we open each session of Qi Gong Practice. It is through this state of being that the inner path is revealed, allowing us to enter into communion with our Soul, Creation, and Christ.

It is my hope and prayer that in sharing the theory of Qi

Gong Practice, it has become clear again to all of us Who We Are:

- We are God
- We are the whole of Creation
- We are Christ

Our identity and our value come from God because God's Love is complete giving. Through God's complete giving, Creation came into being. And it is through God and Creation's complete giving that we, too, came into being. We are Christ, a consciousness and being who, through God's Love, is all of God, is all of Creation, and also is the precious balance created within their union.

As Christ ~
We are all of God ~ the Oneness of God that is beyond all vibrational existence; beyond conceptualization, mind, feeling, space and time. And we are the infinite potential (the infinite beliefs and stories) of God; the source from which all love, life, and vibrational existence comes.

As Christ ~
We are all of Creation ~ the Trinity or *3-in-1 expression* of God Our Mother as the yin Qi, yang Qi, and the Divine Intelligence coordinating the vibrational dance of their giving and receiving of one another. God Our Mother is the vibrational expression of our non-vibrational Father. She is the omniscience, omnipresence, and omnipotence of all vibrational realities, equal to God in all ways except one ~ she is not her own source.

And as Christ ~

We are the children of God and Creation, the Consciousness and Being conceived in the union of our non-vibrational Father (God as our Soul) and our vibrational Mother (Creation as our Etheric, Astral, Causal, and Spiritual Bodies).

- Our Soul is God, the non-vibrational source of all Creation and all life.
- Our Body is the whole of Creation, the Divine Intelligence and vibrational Qi that brings God's Oneness, Love and infinite potential into existence.
- In addition, we are this most precious balance that now exists between God and Creation, between Soul and body, between non-vibration and vibration. This precious balance is the holy Consciousness and Being that we are.

Though We Experience Vibration, We Are Not Vibrational

As this precious balance, we are vibrational and non-vibrational. But the very essence of us is non-vibrational. Remember that all vibrational existence comes out of our non-vibrational source, God, and God within us, our Soul. We are our Soul and we are our Soul's Christ Consciousness, the ability of our Soul to consciously experience all of or any part of God reflected in the Qi of Creation and our body.

And yet, for as long as we choose to consciously experience Creation, our Soul and consciousness will inhabit a vibrational body. Our body ~ spiritual, causal, astral, and etheric, is God Our Mother's gift to us of all of herself. It is through this gift that we can enter Creation and have an individually unique experience of God. But we must experience this holy gift through the wisdom of our precious balance. We must always remember that, though our body is the whole of Creation, it is not our source; it is not where our identity and value come from. When we consciously choose to live our life through this balance, we again experience ourselves as being the consciousness and living expression of God and Creation, while at the same time knowing that we are God. This is the gift, the magic, and the unlimited power of Who We Are.

We are the precious balance that exists between God and Creation, between Soul and body, between non-vibration and vibration... When we consciously choose to live through this balance, we again experience ourselves as being the consciousness and living expression of God and Creation, while at the same time knowing that we are God.

This precious balance is what we have lost and what we must reclaim. The actualization of this balance is our reawakening or enlightenment. It is our time to again know that we are God and God's Christ Consciousness (non-vibrational). It is time for us to know again that we also are the whole of Creation (vibrational), while remembering that the one source of all Creation and all life is God. Our core truth is then undeniably clear: We are God. This is our remembrance; this is our precious balance.

We have come to know that our precious balance is eternally held for us in God. And we now know that we need but ask God for help and guidance to again be the Christ Consciousness and Being existing as this balance.

We have also come to understand that our life is about the relationships connecting our Soul, consciousness, and body for we are the union of all three of them. This is the metaphysical knowledge we receive through the practice. But even more to the point, we are learning to again master the relationship that connects our non-vibrational aspects as Soul and Christ Consciousness with our vibrational aspect as body. It is in this relationship that our precious balance exists.

The radical understanding that is being brought forward here is this:

1. Our Soul (God within us) and our Christ Consciousness are not vibrational.
2. Our Soul and Christ Consciousness are the essence of Who We Are. This is our core truth. The whole of Creation and our body are vibrational reflections of *Who We Are and/or who we believe we are.*
3. Our present consciousness (who we now believe we are) becomes vibrational, and hence has different levels and qualities, to the extent that we are choosing to attach our identity and value to the Qi of Creation and our body, and to the extent that we are choosing to attach our

identity and value to our experiences of the vibrational reflections in the Qi of the beliefs we presently hold as our truth.

Our Soul and our Christ Consciousness are not vibrational. We become vibrational to the extent that we choose to attach our identity and value to the Qi of Creation and our body, and to our experiences of the vibrational reflections in the Qi.

Another way to state this is the less we attach our identity and value to the Qi and to our experiences of the vibrational reflections in the Qi,

- The higher is our consciousness,
- The more expanded is our consciousness,
- OR IN TRUTH, THE LESS VIBRATIONAL IS OUR CONSCIOUSNESS.

The vibrational reflections of the beliefs we are choosing to identify with and hold on to as our truth have become our reality, and it is our choosing to hold on to them that makes it so. But in God's truth, our Soul and consciousness can never be vibrational. For in God there is no separation or limitation, there are no levels, there is nothing to give to or receive from. God is Oneness.

The Essence Movement Is the Application of
The Keys for the Transformation of Human Consciousness

In our prayer to God (The Qi Gong State), we are asking to come home, to return to the Oneness and Love of God that we are and have always been. In response, God is reminding us, through our Central Altar and the Qi of all Creation, that we are the ultimate Christ Consciousness of God uniting the One Spirit of God, Creation, all consciousness, and all life.

We are always sensing God, and the most direct route to God is to intend our consciousness back to our Soul (God within us). This is the deep meditation practice and, hands down, the most effective practice we can do to know again our oneness with God.

The only thing is, we, as consciousness are still attached to the Qi of our mind (thoughts), heart (feelings and emotions), and body (energy and matter). And we are attached to our experiences of the reflections of God that we are choosing to experience in these vibrational levels. Any attempt to direct our consciousness to our Soul involves our releasing or letting go of these attachments.

It is for this purpose that God, through the Qi of Creation and our body and with the help of Christ, is revealing to us the inner path. Along the way, they are now showing us how to apply *The Keys for the Transformation of Human Consciousness* in order that we may release these attachments. The application of these keys within the sacred altars of our temple is the Essence Movement of Qi Gong Practice.

It is our experience of the Essence Movement within the vibrational layers of our body that defines the different levels or types of Qi Gong Practice:

- In **Etheric Qi Gong Practice**, we are working with the Qi of energy and matter through the Lower Tan Tien, the Etheric Altar of our being.
- In **Astral Qi Gong Practice**, we work with the Qi of feeling and emotions through the Middle Tan Tien, the Astral Altar of our being.
- And in **Causal Qi Gong Practice**, we work with the Qi of thoughts and intentions through the Upper Tan Tien, the Causal Altar of our being.

As we walk this path deeper into ourselves, the practice of Qi Gong becomes spiritual, regardless of the level on which we experience it. The practice is always moving us into the Oneness of God that transcends all separation and all levels. In the Essence Movement, we are trusting and allowing the yin and yang forces of Qi to form balance (the reflection of God's Oneness in Creation) within each of our altars ~ Causal, Astral, and Etheric. In the Core Event these three altars then reunite to become one altar. This one altar is our Central Altar and Spiritual Body.

So here I reiterate. This inner path and the language through which we receive the guidance and help of God, God Our Mother (Creation), and Christ is Qi Gong Practice. Our letting go of the attachments we have formed by applying the Keys for the Transformation of Human Consciousness is The Essence Movement of Qi Gong Practice. And to where this path leads us, our conscious experience of Who We Are, is <u>The Core Event of Qi Gong Practice</u>.

I discussed what the Core Event is in chapter 7. In this event, we are accessing the Central Altar of our temple and, if you will remember, our Central Altar is our Spiritual Body.

Our Spiritual Body is also formed from Qi, though this Qi is God Our Mother in her natural state of supreme balance. In this state of balance, God Our Mother is the Preheaven Qi spoken of in Qi Gong theory and Traditional Chinese Medicine. It is in our Spiritual Body, formed from Preheaven Qi, that we consciously experience the pure reflection of our Soul.

The Core Event of Qi Gong Practice is our enlightenment; it is our return to Christ Consciousness, it is our conscious experience of being the Oneness and Love unifying God, Creation, and Christ. This Core Event, which takes place within our human temple, arises naturally from the Essence Movement.

Through The Essence Movement, We Neutralize Our Separation

The Essence Movement of Qi Gong Practice takes place at the interface of consciousness and Creation. If you will remember, the sacred altars of our temple form this interface. They are the portals by which our non-vibrational consciousness experiences vibrational

Creation. It is here then, within our altars, that we apply the Keys for the Transformation of Human Consciousness.

We are practicing how to experience vibrational existence while knowing that we do not come from these experiences.

As we apply the four keys of Allowance, Trust, Surrender, and Non-attachment to Outcome, to all of our experiences on every level of our reality, we are practicing how to experience vibrational existence while knowing that we do not come from these experiences. We are remembering that our identity and value do not come from the Qi or from the reflections of God in the Qi. This practice is how we let go of that which stands between God and us ~ it is the neutralization of our separation from God.

I believe that Pantanjali, the revered sage of Raja Yoga (the royal, yogic path that unites man with God) and the author of The Yoga Sutras, was referring to this neutralization when he defined yoga practice as being "the neutralization of the alternating waves in consciousness". I believe that Pantanjali, in this definition of yoga, is talking about the non-vibrational/vibrational interface of our consciousness with Creation. I believe he is telling us that the practice of Yoga, like the practice of Qi Gong, is a path for reclaiming the precious balance of Christ Consciousness as we navigate this interface.

Our consciousness, Christ Consciousness, does not consist of "alternating waves". It does not come from vibration nor can it be defined by vibration. And yet, our consciousness can experience the reflection of God (or any facet of God we choose) in the alternating waves or vibrating Qi of Creation.

The essence of Who We Are is not vibrational. We are God, and we are God's Christ Consciousness. As Christ, we are God's ability to experience the vibrational reflection of any part of itself (or its entirety) as the infinite, vibrational realities of Creation. Also remember that as Christ, we've been given the gift of choice. We can consciously experience any part of God, any of the infinite beliefs of God, as our vibrational reality. It has been through our choice to believe that we come from the Qi, and from our experiences of the reflections of God in the Qi, that our consciousness has become bound to the Qi. In other words, our non-vibrational consciousness now experiences itself as being vibrational because of the beliefs we are choosing to hold on to as our truth.

The wisdom shared here is that to be the precious balance of Christ; to be God and Creation, and the witnessing consciousness of and for both, we have to remember that absolutely everything we experience in Creation comes out of our Soul. We are the creator of everything, and we are who chooses what we consciously experience.

In this remembering we reclaim Who We Are ~ the Christ Consciousness and Being who is God, who is the whole of Creation, and who is the living wisdom that knows and demonstrates that all vibrational realities come out of our non-vibrational God Self. This wisdom is the preciousness of our precious balance.

As we begin to accept Who We Are and again recognize that our identity and value do not come from Creation, Qi, nor from our experiences of the reflections in the Qi of the beliefs we are choosing, we are ready. We are ready to receive the keys for our transformation and to be guided in the application of them.

Trust, Allowance, Surrender, and Non-Attachment to Outcome are the four Keys for the Transformation of Human Consciousness. Applying these keys to each and every experience of our life is the method of our awakening; it is the Essence Movement by which our consciousness withdraws its identity and value from vibrational existence. As we start to live through these keys, we literally are placing our hands on the steering wheel of our spiritual life. These keys show us how to navigate in a healthy way the non-vibrational/ vibrational interface of our consciousness with Creation.

The Core Act of
The Essence Movement Is to Let Go

The primary action that occurs within the Essence Movement is simple. It is to release and let go. In this act, we, as consciousness, choose to let go of the attachments we have formed to the Qi, and we choose to let go of the attachments we have formed to our experiences of the reflections of God in the Qi. These reflections are the beliefs and stories within God that we are choosing to hold on to as our truth.

What we are experiencing in the Qi of our reality now (though not everything) does not portray the Oneness and Love of God. We are presently experiencing only pieces of God, and even in those pieces, we are not seeing, feeling or touching God's Totality and God's Oneness. The cause of this is two fold: It is because of the specific pieces of God (the beliefs based in separation and limitation) we are choosing to hold as our truth (and of course, what guides us in making these choices is who we believe we are), and it is because of the disturbances we cause in the balance of the yin Qi and yang Qi forces that bring forth all of Creation and our body. We are causing these disturbances through the way we attach to the Qi and to the reflections manifesting within her.

But as we move deeper into ourselves on the inner path, our sense of God's Oneness and Love strengthens, and who we believe we are changes. We no longer feel impelled to judge and manipulate the Qi of Creation. This leads us to stop identifying with what we are now experiencing in the Qi and to cease holding on to these experiences as our truth. We also begin to choose different beliefs, beliefs that portray God's essence. As a result of these changes within us, we again trust and allow God Our Mother to form her supreme balance. Within her we experience anew the pure image of our God Self.

What we are actually letting go of as we play out the Essence Movement within our altars is our attachment

We are letting go of our identification with any thought, feeling, emotion, attitude, behavior, and expression of energy and matter that does not portray God's wholeness and complete sharing of self (love).

to and identification with any vibrational reflection; any thought, feeling, emotion, attitude, behavior, and expression of energy or matter that does not portray God's wholeness and complete sharing of self (love). In the higher expressions of this movement, we, as consciousness, are choosing to let go of beliefs – all beliefs that are not the whole of God and the complete giving of God, all beliefs that do not carry God's quality of Oneness and Love. All of this letting go is done, of course, with the guidance and help of God, God Our Mother, and Christ.

Though it is by no means a complete list, I want to again name the primary beliefs we have been choosing, and the subsequent reflections of these beliefs that we are presently experiencing. It is these beliefs and their reflections that we must let go of, thus ceasing to acquire our identity and value from them:

1. There exists a power that opposes God.
2. We are separate from God, each other, all life forms, and all things.
3. We are limited in our power to love (our ability

to share ourselves) and limited in our power to manifest our will.

4. Our identity and value come from the Qi of Creation, and from our experiences of the reflections in the Qi of the pieces God that we have chosen to hold on to as our truth.

5. We must judge our experiences. We must judge them according to what we believe is right and wrong, good and bad, beautiful and ugly, etc. And we must judge them according to our beliefs about how the beings and things around us can benefit and augment us, or hurt and diminish us.

6. We must control and manipulate Creation (the Qi), and we must take from her in order to be whole, and to find purpose and meaning.

God Our Mother
Brings God into Our Experience

We choose to embark on this path of internal practice and apply the transformational keys to our experiences of life because we want to awaken. We feel impelled to remember Who We Are as both the whole of Christ and the individually, unique part of this whole that we have chosen to express here and now.

The absolute totality of us is in our Soul, for our Soul is God. And yet, as we already know, God Our Mother brings absolutely all of this information into the whole of Creation and our body. This is her "gong", her work or purpose. God Our Mother in her natural state of supreme balance is the vibrational expression of God. She is the vibrational counterpart of Oneness and Love. Her Qi, in this state of supreme balance, is the Preheaven or Prenatal Qi that forms our Spiritual Body.

Because we have been given God's unlimited power (free will), we can also experience pieces of God. These fragments of God are what we are presently choosing to hold on to as our truth... Our identity and value, our truth, can come only from God's wholeness and unlimited power.

The reflections of God and our Soul that we can experience in the Preheaven Qi of our Spiritual Body and Creation are holographic. Each and every part of Creation and our body does contain the whole of God. As we allow and trust the Qi to be in her natural state, we, as consciousness, do again experience the pure reflection of God and our Soul within her. Trusting and allowing the Qi to form this supreme balance within the sacred altars of our temple is the main intention in the Essence Movement. Remember, trust and allowance are the first two keys we employ in the transformation of our consciousness.

We can reawaken. We, as Christ, can consciously experience the pure reflection of our Soul (God) in our Spiritual Body. In this experience (The Core Event), we again know God, Creation, and our consciousness to be one thing. Because we have been given all of God and, therefore, God's unlimited power (free will), we can also experience pieces of God. These fragments of God are what we are presently choosing to hold on to as **our truth**. Remember, it is who we believe we are that guides us in choosing the parts of God we consciously experience.

This is why remembering Who We Are and reclaiming our precious balance is the primary intention of Qi Gong Practice. What we have forgotten is that we are all of God; we are the Oneness and Love of God. Our identity and value, our truth, can come only from God's Wholeness and unlimited Power.

Even Now We Are Experiencing God

In spite of our forgetting, we still often experience the Oneness and Love of God reflected in the Qi of our reality. These experiences come out of our sense of an interconnecting oneness running throughout Creation and our sense of infinity and eternity. We experience vibrational reflections of God's Oneness and Love in the following:

- **Equality** – Our seeing the sanctity and equal importance of each part of Creation, and therefore our treating each life form and thing with reverence.
- **Inclusion** – Our seeing and accepting every expression of life and aspect of Creation as part of ourselves and therefore excluding nothing.
- **Unlimited Potential** – Our seeing the infinite potential of God in everything, and therefore offering our help and guidance to each life form and part of Creation in its evolution in consciousness.

I believe that we, as the family of Christ, have passed the critical point in our transformation of consciousness and perceptual change. We are again seeking to know God, Creation, and Who We Are, and we are seeking to know the nature of our relationship to God, Creation, and each other. We see evidence to this effect in the environmental movement, rapid advances in global communication, and in the movements toward holism in health care, economics, social reform, many branches of science, and the movement for world peace.

Trust

OUR TRUST BEGINS WITH AND is built upon the foundation of our acceptance of God and Creation and ourselves as Christ. This acceptance is an essential part in the Qi Gong State of Acceptance, Gratitude, and Invitation. Without this foundation of acceptance, we have no starting point for our journey. We would not have a conception of who and what we trust and believe in. We would not be able to conceptualize their and our potential, nor could we believe in their and our ability to act on and make real this potential. It is upon this acceptance that we build trust!

It is for this purpose that the metaphysical knowledge about God (the Oneness, Love, and infinite potential of God), about God Our Mother (the Divine Intelligence and Qi of Creation), and about us (the Christ Consciousness and Being) is now being shared. This is also why this knowledge has been the major focus of this discourse.

We start the practice of Qi Gong in our deepest sense of God (our connection to Soul via the Central Altar) and

Our trust forms the basis of our courage to let go of what we are presently choosing to experience as real. This letting go is the essential act we do in each of the four keys.

in our present experiences of the reflections of God's Oneness and Love in the Qi of our thoughts, feelings, and perceptions of energy and matter. It is our trust in the following that opens us and motivates us to receive and act on the guidance and help being given to us by God and Christ through the Qi of God Our Mother:

- Our sense of God
- What we believe God, Creation, and we are
- Our experiences of the vibrational reflections of God's Oneness and Love that even now, we are having
- The potential and the actualizing ability in them and us

Without this trust, we cannot effectively apply the transformational keys to our experiences of life. In much the same way that our acceptance is the foundation of our trust, our trust forms the basis of our courage; the courage to let go of what we are presently choosing to experience as real, and who we are presently choosing to believe we are. Remember, this letting go of what we have chosen to attach to is the essential act we do in each of the four keys, including the first key of trust. For even in our trust, we are letting go of our attachment to fear.

Each step of Qi Gong Practice is this letting go of our attachments ~ our attachments to who we have believed we are, and our attachments to our experiences of the vibrational reflections of these beliefs. In many ways each letting go, no matter on which level it takes place or through which key it happens, feels like a death, because we presently feel that these beliefs and experiences form us and are us. But Qi Gong Practice is also another kind of letting go ~ it is our choice to release or give ourselves, through trust, to the Divine Intelligence, Power, and Love that is creating and sustaining all of existence. This releasing or letting go of ourselves is the key of Surrender, the third transformational key. In this way, our letting go is like many rebirths.

Our trust is in God and God within us as our Soul. It is in Creation, her Divine Intelligence and Qi. And our trust is in ourselves, the Christ Consciousness and Being:

- We are trusting God to hear our prayer to awaken, trusting that God is responding to our prayer and guiding us back into the Oneness and Love we share with God (the Oneness and Love that we have forgotten we are).
- We are trusting Creation to orchestrate through her Divine Intelligence the supreme balance, the balance in her yin and yang Qi that receives God and brings God's reflection into vibrational

existence. We are trusting her to make real to us God's answer to our prayer that it may become our new reality.

- We are trusting our brothers and sisters in Christ, those of us that have walked this path before and who have returned now to help us.
- We are trusting ourselves, who also are Christ, to form the prayer of our salvation. We are trusting ourselves to receive God's answer to our prayer as it comes to us through the Qi of Creation, and trusting ourselves to have the courage to follow God, Creation and Christ's guidance and help as we walk this inner path.

IN EACH TRANSFORMATIONAL KEY, our movement is always to let go into oneness. The movement is always toward the Oneness and Love of God that transcends (neutralizes) separation, regardless of the vibrational level of Creation in which we experience it.

The majority of our letting go happens in this key, the key of Allowance, and in the next, the key of Surrender. The difference between these two keys is what we let go of. In the transformational key of Surrender, it is ourselves, our consciousness and whom we believe we are, that we release unto God and unto the union of supreme balance that naturally forms in the Qi. But in this key, the transformational key of Allowance, what we are letting go of is the kind of relationship we have chosen to be in with the Qi of Creation, and with the reflections we are experiencing in her.

Let me describe the movement of allowance in more detail. As we remember that our identity and value do not come from Creation, we choose to let go of our attachments

In the key of Allowance, we let go of the kind of relationship we have chosen to be in with the Qi and with the reflections we experience in her.

to both expressions of Qi, the yin Qi force and the yang Qi force. We also choose to let go of our attachments to both the yin side and the yang side of each reflection we experience in the Qi on every vibrational level of Creation ~ Causal, Astral, and Etheric.

We let go of our attachments by letting go of judging what we experience and our belief that we need to judge. We also do this by letting go of controlling and manipulating the Qi and the reflections in the Qi, and our belief that we need to control and manipulate them.

If you will remember, it is through our acts of judgement (ch. 10, pp 156, 163-165) and our acts of control and manipulation (ch. 5, p 63, also ch. 10, pp 156-158) that we attach to the Qi and to the reflections of God that we have chosen to consciously experience. When we attach our identity and value to either the yin or the yang side of our experiences, we are binding our consciousness to the experience of both sides and to the reality in which they exist.

As we so very well know, Creation and our bodies are not currently reflecting to us what God is and Who We Are ~ the unifying Oneness of God and the infinite

Power to love. And as I've stated before, this is not the fault of the Qi; it is not the Qi that must change. For us to again experience the pure reflection of God and the pure reflection of our Soul, we, as consciousness, must change our relationship with the Qi and with the reflections we are presently experiencing within her.

The formation of the supreme balance in the yin and yang forces of Qi by the Divine Intelligence of God Our Mother on all three levels of Creation, which also are the three altars of our human temple, is the natural way. The integration or harmonization of the three levels of Creation and the three altars of our being into the vibrational counter part of God's Oneness is the spiritual form of Creation and our own Spiritual Body (The Core Event). This harmonization is the natural process that wants to happen.

It is only our consciousness that is impeding these processes. In our choice to attach our consciousness to the divided perceptions we are now experiencing in Creation (within ourselves and, therefore, outside ourselves as well), we stop the natural movement toward Oneness and Love. So, as we choose to no longer seek our identity and value from Creation by not judging our experiences of her on any level, and by not controlling and manipulating her on any level, we release the tethers that bind our consciousness to the ongoing play of opposites. These opposites are the yin and yang forces inherent to every aspect of our present reality and forming the two sides of every experience we are now having. We realize again that our identity and value never did come from the Qi or from our experiences of the reflections within the Qi. We remember our precious balance (ch. 2 pp 31-32, ch. 5 pp 59-63, ch. 13 pp 196-198), which is intimately linked to the supreme balance within God Our Mother. In our letting go, we are allowing God Our Mother to do what she was created to do ~ form the supreme balance, the vibrational manifestation of God's Oneness and Love in the yin and yang Qi forces of Creation.

No longer encumbered by our meddling in her divine work, her gong, God Our Mother gives to us the conscious experience of our own God Self. Our consciousness is then freed from its self-caused entrapment within a vibrational reality of our separation from God, and our limitation to love.

The greatest untruth we have chosen to believe in is that there exists a power that opposes God. When we accept this belief as our truth, it becomes a part of who we believe we are. We therefore experience that a part of us also opposes God.

Who we believe we are is what guides us in choosing, from the infinite beliefs and stories within God, which beliefs we will consciously experience. So it is easy to see how the influences of this untruth find their way into and become an integral part of all the other beliefs we choose. All of these beliefs are, of course, received by the Qi of Creation and our bodies to become our reality.

And so it is that our choice to believe in a power that works in opposition to God causes everything in our reality to appear to us as if it existed separate from God and us, and separate from every other thing. It is also this belief that causes everything in our reality to appear to us as if it were composed of two opposing sides.

Every reflection of God in every realm of Creation... our thoughts within the Causal, our feelings and emotions within the Astral, and our perceptions of energy and matter within the Etheric... is experienced by us as having opposing sides, a yin side and a yang side. This is the divided nature or duality of our present world. Every thought only has meaning in relativity to a complementary or comparative thought. Every feeling and emotion has two opposing sides. Every expression of energy is a sine wave (~) formed from peaks and troughs. And every atom and molecule is formed in opposing electro-magnetic charges (+ and -).

If we think it, feel it, or see-hear-smell-taste-touch it, we will think, feel, see-hear-smell-taste-touch its opposite.
- If you know something, you will experience not knowing it.
- If you fear this, you will not fear it. And if you don't fear it, you will sometime fear it.
- To have anything is to experience not having it.
- To not do something is to experience doing it.

- To be something (like being a Qi Gong Teacher) is to also not be it (I am not a Qi Gong Teacher).
- And finally, because we attach to life, we experience death, and because we believe in death, we continue to be reborn into the experience of life.

When we choose to attach our consciousness to the yang side of any experience (thought, feeling, or thing) we make real the yin, and we will then also experience the yin side. And when we attach our consciousness to the yin, the yang becomes real to us, and we will then also experience the yang side.

Out of the untruth that there exists a power that opposes God arises yet another profound untruth that we have also chosen to believe in: *We can achieve God or earn our way into the infinity and eternity of heaven by choosing to think, feel, be, or do what we experience as the right or good thing, and by not thinking, feeling, being, or doing what we perceive to be the wrong or bad thing.* Hidden within this untruth are the beliefs that we must therefore judge our every experience, and we must control and manipulate them to our benefit.

In our choice to hold on to these beliefs as our truth, and through each act we do in this life that is motivated by these beliefs, we not only cause the opposing sides of our experiences, but we also bind our consciousness to the ongoing experience of both. If we so choose, we can be and not be, have and not have, live and die, forever.

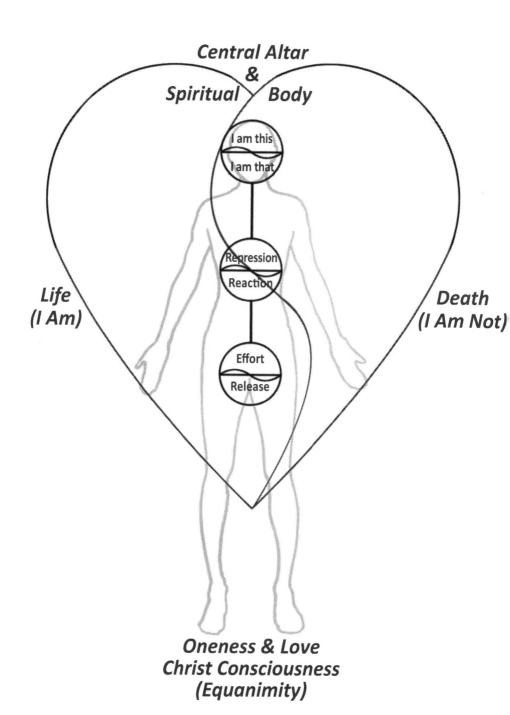

Central Altar
&
Spiritual Body

I am this
I am that

Life
(I Am)

Death
(I Am Not)

Repression
Reaction

Effort
Release

Oneness & Love
Christ Consciousness
(Equanimity)

The Maps of Our Altars

Causal Altar

Spirit and Our Soul ~ Mind of God

Upper Tan Tien •   • Altar of Awareness
                      and Choice

Causal Body •   • Center of Thought

Mental Body •   • Conceptualization and
                   Visualization

Brain •   • Meaning

           • Design

           • Decision

           • Intention

           • Identity and Value

           • Judgement

           • Control and
             Manipulation

The Dualities

I am this	I am that
Future	Past
Here	There
Believing	Not believing
Knowing	Not knowing
I do this	I don't do this (I do that)
I have this	I don't have this (I have that)
Success	Failure
Good	Bad
Right	Wrong

Allowing Balance

1. While being aware of and experiencing all Creation, we choose not to identify with (not seek our identity and value from) either the yin or yang side of any experience.
2. We choose to be and to live our life in the present moment.
3. We trust and allow the yin and yang expressions of our thoughts to flow into each other to form the union of supreme balance that leads us into transformation.
4. We practice choiceless awareness (Qi Gong meditation).
5. We hold the space of not knowing and not having to understand.
6. We release our attachments to the world's definitions and measurements of success and failure.
7. We let go of our perceived need to judge our experiences.
8. We let go of our need to control and manipulate the objects and beings of our experiences.

Characteristics of Causal Balance

1. Awareness of Oneness ~ Christ Consciousness.
2. Living in the eternal access to God ~ the present moment.
3. Living through a mind that is informed by our Central Altar (our Spiritual Body), a mind that is a clear reflection of the oneness and unlimited power we share with God and all Creation.
4. Imagination and creativity.
5. As we hold the space (the spaciousness) of not knowing and not having to understand, we more fully open ourselves to God and Creation; we stop limiting what we can receive from God, God Our Mother, and Christ.
6. The experiences of insight, revelation, and transformation.

Astral Altar

Consciousness ~ Heart of God

Middle Tan Tien •	• Altar of Interrelation
Astral Body •	• Communication (Carrier of Information)
Emotional Body •	• Interaction
Heart •	• Center of feeling and emotion
	• Attention (Mover of Qi)
	• Concentration and focus
	• Nerves, hormones, neurotransmitters, neuropeptides
	• The extraordinary opening to our Soul that permits us to sense our oneness with God, Creation, and each other
	• Informs our Causal Altar of the ways we, as Consciousness, can interrelate with Creation and each other

The Dualities

Reaction	Repression
Desire	Fear
Attraction	Repulsion
Acceptance	Rejection
Giving	Receiving
Pleasure	Pain

Allowing Balance

1. We allow our feelings to arise within us.
2. We truly feel our feelings and emotions, holding them in the light of our conscious mind without reaction to them (using them as the impetus for unconscious action) or repressing them.
3. We allow the yin and yang expressions of our feelings and emotions to flow into each other.
4. We trust and allow the Divine Intelligence of God Our Mother to reunite the yin and yang sides of each feeling and emotion in the union of supreme balance.
5. We trust and allow the timing of God Our Mother.

Characteristics of Astral Balance

1. Unconditional love
2. Emotional equanimity
3. Joy
4. Compassion and empathy
5. Forgiveness (of ourselves and others)

Etheric Altar

Creation ~ Body of God

Lower Tan Tien •   • Altar of Actualization

Etheric Body •   • Center of Movement (Action)

Physical Body •   • Storehouse of Qi

Kidneys/Adrenals •   • Adaptation to our Environment

   • Anatomy and Physiology of the Physical Body (organ systems)

The Dualities

Effort	Release
Doing	Non-Doing
Tension	Relaxation
Expand	Contract
Open	Close
Rise	Sink
Move Forward	Move Back
Move Right	Move Left
Spiral Right	Spiral Left
Outside	Inside

Allowing Balance

1. We allow the Etheric expressions of yin Qi and yang Qi to simultaneously express and flow into each other.
2. We trust and allow the yin and yang forces of Qi to form a union of supreme balance.
3. We release our perceived need to control the movements born from this union.

Characteristics of Etheric Balance

1. Effortless movement, a sense of being carried by Qi
2. Access to the Etheric Web that embraces all of the expressions of energy and matter
3. Stillness, the state of "being"
4. Sensitivity
5. Power
6. Physical health

The essence of this key is beautifully shared in Psalms 139, verses 7-12:

- Whither shall I go from thy spirit? Or whither shall I flee from thy presence?
- If I ascend up into heaven, thou art there: if I make my bed in hell, behold thou art there
- If I take the wings of the morning, and dwell in the uttermost parts of the sea:
- Even there shall thy hand lead me, and thy right hand shall hold me.
- If I say, surely the darkness shall cover me; even the night shall be light about me.
- Yea, the darkness hideth not from thee; but the night shineth as the day: the darkness and light are both alike to thee.

We have been created to experience God in all Creation and in all life. We were not created to become entrapped within any one reality. So, in this key, God, God Our Mother, and Christ are showing us that every one of our experiences of this reality is made up from two opposing sides, a yin side and a yang side. Then, as they remind us that we are God's Oneness and God's Love, they are guiding and helping us to stop attaching our identity and value to either the yin or yang side of our experiences. We do this by choosing to not judge, control, or manipulate our experiences. In this choice, we allow the yin side and the yang side of our experiences to flow into each other, forming the union of supreme balance. It is in this balance that our consciousness is initiated into the experience of our Soul's reflection and truly begins to know freedom.

We simply are being guided to choose again. We are being shown that there never existed nor could there ever exist a power that opposes God. And we are being shown the effects of our believing in such a power ~ the experience of a reality founded on separation and limitation in which we forever cycle through birth and death, growth and decay, having and not having, happiness and sadness, knowing and not knowing, etc. And finally, God, through Creation and the collective wisdom of Christ, is calling us back home.

This calling coincides with the new dispensation, the Spiritual Intelligence of the Aquarian Age. In order for us to receive this guidance and help, we need but let go of our attachments to the now obsolete beliefs and acts of our Piscean past. Those beliefs and the experiences they spawned, though they taught us much about who we are not, do not serve us anymore. Even the spiritual practices based in those beliefs must now be let go of, for their usefulness has expired.

There is nothing to overcome, there is nothing separating us from God, Creation, and each other. There is not a "Lower Self" opposing a "Higher Self" or an ego fighting against God for its very existence. Our "lower chakras" are not in opposition to our heart and the "upper chakras". And the tan tiens, the sacred altars of our temple, are not separate from one another.

We are now in the time of oneness, the time of Christ's return. We are right now being shown how to trust and allow all of the pieces and levels of ourselves, all of the pieces and levels of Creation, and all of the life forms inhabiting our reality, to come back into the Oneness of God.

There is not a "Lower Self" opposing a "Higher Self" or an ego fighting against God for its very existence. Our "lower chakras" are not in opposition to our heart and the "upper chakras". And the sacred altars of our temple are not separate from one another.

In the instructional manuals and DVDs that supplement this book I will share how we, as we consciously choose to stop seeking out and acquiring our identity and value from the Qi and from what we now experience in her, allow the yin and yang sides of our experiences to flow into one another. This is the essence of Qi Gong Practice. I will also share how this practice manifests in all three vibrational planes of Creation and our body. These three levels of Qi Gong Practice, Causal, Astral and Etheric, are also touched on in *The Maps of Our Three Sacred Altars and Their Dualities* (ch. 15, pp 226-232) in the sections called Allowing Balance.

I cannot leave this key without including one more powerful and essential part of Allowance ~ we must allow ourselves to be human. In order to not obstruct our own awakening, we must allow ourselves to be where we are on the inner path; we must not judge the person we believe we are now.

When we judge ourselves, we also are judging what we experience in the world around us ~ as it is within, so it is without. So it only goes to say that as we stop judging ourselves, we stop judging what is happening in our reality. We are then able to allow the opposing sides of our experiences to flow into each other to form the union of supreme balance.

Divine Intelligence guides us to stop judging, controlling, and manipulating our experiences. But we must, at the same time, forgive ourselves even as we continue to bind our consciousness to Creation by our acts of judgement, control, and manipulation. This forgiveness appears in our experiences as we live our life through the transformational keys. It is a natural part of our remembering. It is only through this forgiveness of ourselves that we can truly forgive the imbalances of our world.

We are God and God's witnessing consciousness. Who We Are did not come from and cannot ever come from what we believe we have done in Creation, nor from what we believe has been done to us. Moreover, as we choose to no longer judge ourselves, we allow Creation to be what she has always been ~ the pure reflection of God's Oneness and Love.

WE HAVE ALL PRAYED. In our prayers, we have asked God to guide and help us so that we can remember Who We Are, and again be the living expression of Christ in our every experience of Creation.

In the first transformational key, we choose to trust God. We trust that God hears us and is giving to us, through the Qi of Creation, absolutely everything we need to reawaken.

In the second key, we are choosing to allow the Divine Intelligence and Power of God Our Mother, the Qi, to bring God's answer to us. This we do by no longer interfering in her divine work, her gong. We revere her mastery; we choose to stop judging, controlling, and manipulating her.

And now we come to the third key, the key of Surrender. At this juncture, we choose to surrender our consciousness and all that we have believed we are into the unknown, into what we have not yet seen or comprehended. This step requires all of our courage for we are walking away from everything we have been shown to be real and experienced as real. This is the step onto the unknown path that takes us to what we still do not know. This is the literal act of our transformation.

We choose to surrender our consciousness and all that we have believed we are into the unknown... We release ourselves onto the deeper truth of Who We Are... We surrender into a new way of being on this earth.

In this act of transformation, we are choosing to participate in the ceremony of salvation we have asked for. Each time we make this step, we open ourselves to receive God's help and guidance and truly allow the experiences brought before us through God Our Mother to teach us.

The unknown into which we surrender ourselves is the reflection of God's Oneness and Love within Creation. It is also the reflection of our Soul. This reflection arises from and is experienced by us in the union of opposites, the union of supreme balance that forms as we allow the yin and yang forces of Qi and the yin and yang sides inherent to each of our experiences to flow into each other uninterrupted. If you will remember, this union always seeks to occur and happens naturally wherever and whenever we trust and allow God Our Mother to do her work.

As we move forward on our path, we are continually reminded and shown that our identity and value do not come from any of these experiences. They simply are pointing us toward the one, ever-existing truth ~ we are the Oneness and Love eternally unifying God, Creation, and all consciousness.

So what does it really mean in our everyday lives to surrender, to give ourselves to the Oneness and Love of God as it manifests in Creation? How do we live surrender? Does it mean that we just give up all responsibility, stop caring, and lose ourselves to nothingness? Absolutely not. Our practice of surrender is not a giving up or withdrawing from participating in life, but rather a deeper "listening" or sensing of our Soul. It is a honing or refining of our ability to sense what love is and what the Oneness of God looks and feels like within Creation.

Our practice is also a honing of our discernment. The Divine Intelligence of Creation is teaching us how to invest our time and infinite power. Through our experiences, we are coming to know again which beliefs, of the infinite beliefs and stories of God, hold the totality of Oneness and Love. We are then able to choose these beliefs as our truth. In our growing wisdom, we again become the conscious broker that facilitates the transactions of love between God and Creation. We again become the conscious completion of their love for each other.

The surrender of our consciousness and who we believe we are is a difficult thing to face, for this key is really talking about faith. It is about our trusting in and our giving ourselves to the intelligence and power that creates us and is, as we speak, sustaining our very existence. We have lived a very long time in the consciousness of separation and limitation, losing our conscious knowing that we are this infinite power and the intelligence of this power. We are its design and its function. When we surrender, this is what we fall into. We do not fall into nothing; we release ourselves into the deeper truth of Who We Are. We are love. We are the creative force of the universe that is showing up in us right now as our unique expression of God with its particular form, gifts, preferences, expression of intelligence, and way of loving. When we surrender, it is into our own Soul stream, pregnant with all that we uniquely are, that we fall.

Our transformation happens through God Our Mother; she is Creation, she is the Qi, she is the intelligence, power, and physical body of God. In the practice of Qi Gong, we are availing ourselves of the tremendous influx of Qi that is moving through the earth at this time. This Qi is currently transforming the consciousness of the earth and all life on it. The Great Ones knew that this influx was coming and have been preparing the earth and her inhabitants for the last 2,000 years, the duration of the Piscean Age.

We still, of course, have a choice. We can move with this new dispensation, or we can continue holding on to the old ways of thinking, feeling, being, and doing. These old ways have come out of the belief that there is a power in opposition to God and our choosing to hold this belief as our truth. This belief has authored our present reality, a reality of separation and limitation in which we believe we must judge and overcome our "lower nature" to find God. In this reality we experience infinite opposites and therefore cycle continually through the experiences of life and death.

Well, as the saying goes, "transformation happens". This is a most beautiful time to be alive on this earth. We quite literally are living in a miracle, so I say "let's go with it". And if you and I make this choice, what is it that we actually do? We begin with accepting what is happening in our life now. We give thanks for everything; our existence, our loved ones, all that we've been given, and for the opportunities to learn. And we invite God, God Our Mother, and Christ into our experience of life to guide us and help us remember Who We Are. But ultimately what we do is surrender ourselves into a new way of being on this earth, a new way of relating to Creation. This new way is the Consciousness of Christ, the Consciousness of our Oneness with God, Creation, and all forms of life.

In this Consciousness, we give all of ourselves as an open vessel of God's Love to help and guide all life and all

Creation in its return to God. This surrender is what this transformation is all about.

Because I have made reference to it, I want to close this chapter with a very brief overview of The Precession of The Equinoxes.

A big part of the mystical meaning of the time we are in concerns the entrance of our earth into a new age... The intelligence of this age is informing us that there is no power opposing God.

The Precession of The Equinoxes

An accepted understanding in the practice of astrology, and one that was deeply appreciated in many ancient cultures, is that the position of our earth and solar system in relation to the center of our galaxy plays a central role in the consciousness of man. The ancient astrologers of Egypt, Mexico, and India knew that this relationship between our solar system and the galactic center could be mapped out over a 24,000-year cycle. Basically this means that our solar system returns to the exact same position in its journey through our galaxy every 24,000 years.

In astrology this great cycle is divided into twelve sections, and it takes our solar system approximately 2,000 years to pass through each of them. These twelve sections are the "houses" of the zodiac. The passage of our solar system through all twelve of these areas of space and time is The Precession of the Equinoxes.

On this long journey of 24,000 years, our solar system approaches, passes through, and then leaves a portion of space in which our earth is bathed in a concentrated beam of spiritual power and intelligence (Qi), emanating from the galactic center. The ancients referred to this area of alignment as "Vishnunabhi", the time of direct connection with the One Spirit of God. I am not suggesting that we are now in this alignment, but we have just moved a step closer to it with our departure from the Piscean Age and entrance into the Age of Aquarius.

A big part of the mystical meaning of the time we are in concerns the entrance of our earth into this new age. With this movement, we are receiving a powerful influx of spiritual Qi that is now transforming our consciousness. Each age brings to us the specific intelligence and power we need for those aspects of our God unfoldment we are ready to receive.

And as if you couldn't have guessed, the intelligence of this age is informing us that there is no power opposing God. A path of spiritual unfoldment is now being shared with us ~ the path of oneness. On this path we are being shown again how to recognize this truth and how to allow all of the separate pieces and levels we have believed we are to come back into the Oneness of God.

246

IN MANY WAYS THE LAST KEY, Non-Attachment to Outcome, is the most difficult. From within the belief system we have chosen to hold as our truth, and from within the reality we experience as the reflection of these beliefs, it is hard for us to see that it's all a gift from God. It is God's Love alone that makes everything possible.

Our Soul is God. All Creation and our bodies are God's gift. Our consciousness and all life are God's gift. And our every experience; every what, when, where and how, come from God. And so it is, that even our enlightenment, though it challenges us to receive it, also is a gift from God, extended to us through the intelligence and Qi of Creation.

The dawning of this gift within our consciousness is our first yearning to know Who We Are. This hunger sprouts into our consciousness from the seed of Oneness and Love within us (our Soul) as it is warmed and moistened by the Oneness and Love of Creation. On the grandest level, our yearning is the actualization of God's desire to experience itself. But on our human level, this all plays out through us as God and Creation's way of consciously experiencing the Oneness and Love they share. If you will remember, Christ is God and God Our Mother's ability to consciously experience and love one another.

The tricky part in all of this is that we have forgotten so completely Who We Are. We then chose to attach our identity and value to a set of beliefs and to the manifesting reflections of these beliefs to such an extent, that we now cannot conceptualize, much less experience our truth or how to "attain" it.

As we now clearly understand, the reality we now occupy is the reflection of the belief system we have chosen. And the foundational belief of this system, and therefore the foundation of our reality, is that there exists a power that opposes God. This belief is the primary cause of the duality that is inherent in and permeates our every experience.

Stemming from this belief and our choice to hold this belief as or truth, we experience ourselves as separate from God, Creation, and all life forms, and limited in our power to do anything. In this reality we experience everything outside of us as also being separate and limited, and as having two sides that are in continual opposition to one another. Within this reality of ours, we do not have the materials nor the tools to build the ladder that can lift us beyond separation and limitation. We cannot see God's Oneness and the infinite Power of God's Love through the lenses of our beliefs in separation and limitation.

This is why we need God's guidance and help. This is why our enlightenment must be a gift. We cannot, from within our belief system and the reality it has formed, earn or climb our way into Christ Consciousness. And we surely do not "get there" by repressing or denying any part of ourselves. Our enlightenment is the complete integration of every part of us and every level of us. Anything else is still separation and limitation.

It is important to understand that we do not "earn" enlightenment. We do not reawaken because of what we do. When we believe that our enlightenment comes from anything we do, or will do in the future, we just continue the binding of our consciousness to this reality.

As we receive and then apply the keys of transformation in each and every instant of our life, we experience life through a new, operational system. In this system we trust God, we allow Creation to bring to us God's Love in the form of guidance and help, and we surrender ourselves to the path we have asked for, the path of healing that God has laid out before us in the Qi of Creation.

On this path (The path of Qi Gong Practice), a momentum builds, moving us closer and closer to freedom. The tethers that have bound our consciousness to a reality

When we believe that our enlightenment comes from anything we do, or will do in the future, we just continue the binding of our consciousness to this reality.

of separation and limitation become weaker and weaker as our consciousness becomes less and less vibrational. The power in this momentum is the attraction of Oneness and Love; it is God's response to our prayers now bringing us home.

This momentum begins in each of us as the yearning to know ourselves. Out of this hunger, we ask the three questions:
- Who am I?
- What is my role in this life?
- How am I to live this role?

These questions are the guideposts that lead us to the doorway of our temple. As we enter the Qi Gong State of Acceptance, Gratitude, and Invitation, the door opens, allowing us to step onto the inner path. In this state, we consciously invite God, God Our Mother, and Christ to participate in our life.

On this journey to our center, we are given the Keys for the Transformation of Human Consciousness and the guidance and help we need to apply these keys to each experience of our life. This is The Essence Movement of Qi Gong Practice. We, as consciousness, then stop seeking our identity and value in Creation; we stop acquiring our identity and value from what we are experiencing now within our reality. When we stop judging, controlling, and manipulating Creation, we free her to form the union of supreme balance in the yin and yang Qi of our sacred altars. It is through this balance that she reflects or brings God into vibrational existence.

And finally, this momentum brings us into <u>The Core Event of Qi Gong Practice</u>. No longer impeded by our attachments to her, the Qi forming the three altars of our temple and the three vibrational realms of Creation harmonizes into oneness. In this state of oneness, there does not exist a power that opposes God; there is no force opposing the natural reunification of our altars into our Spiritual Body. Our Spiritual Body is our unified temple and the vibrational expression of Our God Self.

In the Preheaven Qi of our Spiritual Body, we experience the pure reflection of God. In this experience, we consciously know that God, as our Soul, Creation, as our body, and consciousness, our Christ Consciousness, have always been one.

It is here, as we approach our enlightenment, that our path becomes most difficult. We must take great care as we apply the last key of our transformation: Non-Attachment to Outcome. As our consciousness becomes freer and freer, absolutely everything we have held on to as our truth will surface. EVERY FEAR AND DOUBT, WOUND AND HURT, WEAKNESS AND INADEQUACY, will come up into our conscious mind to be experienced on every level of our being. And then, we have a choice ~ will we reengage our "old ways" of experiencing life through judgement, control, and manipulation, or will we continue forward in the momentum of our new operational system, the new way that God is sharing with us through the Qi of God Our Mother.

> *As our consciousness becomes freer, everything we have held on to as our truth will come into our conscious mind to be experienced... As we face all of our greatest fears and an unknown future, we will want to turn back. And turning back is what we are really doing when we attach to any future outcome.*

If we are to truly experience our transformation, we must allow the momentum of our spiritual journey to carry us forward into what we still do not see or know. This momentum is the grace. This is a critical passage for us, for as we face all of our greatest fears and an unknown future, we will want to turn back. And turning back is what we are really doing when we attach to any future outcome. We will want to turn back, not because it serves us, but because it is what we "know" to be real; because we find comfort in what is familiar to us.

It will appear to us that our "old ways" of experiencing life, the ways we have perceived and interacted with life, will give us the solutions we are looking for. And it will appear to us that these ways will be new and different from our past because they are going to happen in our future. But this is not true. This is a great deception. If we, at this point in our awakening, choose to hold on to any particular outcome, we are, without really knowing it, carrying our past into our future. We are actually choosing again to judge, control, and manipulate our experiences, and we are choosing again to seek and acquire our identity and value from our experiences of this reality.

When we choose to hold on to any particular outcome, we are attaching to our past, and we are choosing to not move forward in the momentum of our transformation. Through this act, we continue our attachments to this reality. We continue to bind our consciousness to the experiences of separation and limitation epitomized in the experiences of our birth and death.

Our enlightenment cannot be experienced through our present belief system. And because we, as consciousness, presently define Who We Are and acquire our worth through the experiences of our present reality, we are not able to conceptualize the Oneness and Love of God. Right now we are not experiencing the pure reflection of our Soul in the mirror of Creation and our body. So when we attempt to find enlightenment in a future outcome, we are actually diminishing our ability to receive God's guidance and help. We quite literally get in the way of our own awakening.

As we engage each experience of our life through the transformational keys of Trust, Allowance, and Surrender, we cannot attach to an outcome. In order for us to receive God's gift of Oneness and Love and truly experience our transformation, we have to hold a sacred space of not knowing. We, then, allow God, through the Divine Intelligence and power of Creation, to carry us into this unknown. This is what the key of Non-Attachment to Outcome is asking of us.

ABOUT THE AUTHOR

Lyn Dilbeck is a thirty-year practitioner of Qi Gong and Internal Martial Arts. He currently lives in Sedona, Arizona where he has been teaching these arts for the past twenty years.

To know himself and to help others know themselves has always been the deepest motivating force in Lyn's life. This heart-felt desire is the essence of his Qi Gong Practice and what he shares as a teacher.

Before Lyn started to develop a conscious relationship with Qi through Qi Gong Practice, his quest had taken him into metaphysics and the practice of meditation. Also having a desire to help others, he studied and practiced medicine as a Pediatric and Internal Medicine Physicians Assistant. These earlier studies and life experiences helped him to see that the power and intelligence that give us health is what heals us when we are ill. He felt that this intelligent power must be what sustains every level of our existence ~ physical, energetic, emotional and mental, and it must be connected somehow to the life purpose within each of us.

For Lyn, accepting that health, healing and spirituality were interconnected, was an epiphany that changed the direction of his life. He decided to seek out this intelligent power, to know it within himself, and to help others to know it within themselves.

In the mid-seventies, many people seeking a physical/energetic practice based in spirituality were studying Yoga, Aikido or Tai Qi Chuan. Lyn studied all three forms, yet it was in the practice of the traditional Yang Style of Tai Qi Chuan that he experienced those first "tastes" of a force flowing in and around him.

Lyn has come to know Qi Gong Practice as a conscious conversation between human beings and the Intelligent Power of Creation, Qi. In the course of this conversation he has learned that Qi is the Divine Intelligence and Power that is birthing God's infinite potential into Creation. This is her true gong (purpose), to be the Mother of all vibrational existence and our Mother as well.

Lyn has spent the majority of his life tending this relationship and been fortunate to study with many gifted Masters of Qi Gong and Internal Martial Arts:
• Ralf Cahn, Albany, CA ~ Kang jo fu
• Stephen Labensart, Mt. Shasta, CA ~ Yang Style Tai Qi Chuan
• Lily Soux, Honolulu, HI ~ Qi Gong
• George Xu, San Francisco, CA ~ Chen Style Tai Qi Chuan

- Chris Luth, Solano Beach, CA ~ Push Hands Training
- Master Zhou Ting Jue, Los Angeles, CA ~ Qi Gong (Wu Dang Style), Tai Qi Chuan, Hsing I, Bagua
- Miranda Warburton, Flagstaff, AZ ~ Hsing I, Bagua
- Master Li Jun Feng, Austin, TX ~ Sheng Zhen Qi Gong
- Master Chris Petrilli, Sedona, AZ ~ Escrima

Passionate and generous in all that he shares; Lyn excels in revealing the internal principles of these arts through demonstration and metaphor. His deeper gift however, is the way he shows that these principles are the same keys that allow our true nature to manifest into our life as joy, wisdom, health and love.

In addition to his own practice and teaching, Lyn is a lover of nature. You can often find him on a lake or river, boating and camping. He loves Mexico where he has lived and traveled; he also teaches Spanish as a second language. Lyn is presently working on his second book, an instructional manual and DVD for helping people apply the theory and methods of Qi Gong Practice to their every day life.

FOR MORE INFORMATION about these teachings, acquiring the instructional manuals and DVDs, Lyn's workshops, or hosting a workshop in your area, please contact Lyn via his website: www.spiralinglifeforce.com

17615430R00151

Made in the USA
Charleston, SC
20 February 2013